THE LIVING PARISH

THE LIVING PARISH

A BELIEVING, CARING, PRAYING PEOPLE

JOSEPH M. CHAMPLIN

AVE MARIA PRESS / NOTRE DAME / INDIANA 46556

Acknowledgment:
NC News Service for selected columns published originally in the *Know Your Faith* series, © 1974, 1975, 1976

Nihil Obstat:
>   Rev. John L. Roark
>   Censor Deputatus
>   November 20, 1976

Imprimatur:
>   Most Rev. David F. Cunningham, D.D.
>   Bishop of Syracuse

Library of Congress Catalog Card Number: 76-51887

International Standard Book Number: 0-87793-129-1

© 1977 by Ave Maria Press, Notre Dame, Indiana 46556
All rights reserved. Printed in the United States of America.

Art: Tom Hojnacki

To the members of
HOLY FAMILY PARISH
in Fulton, New York
who truly are
believing, praying, caring people

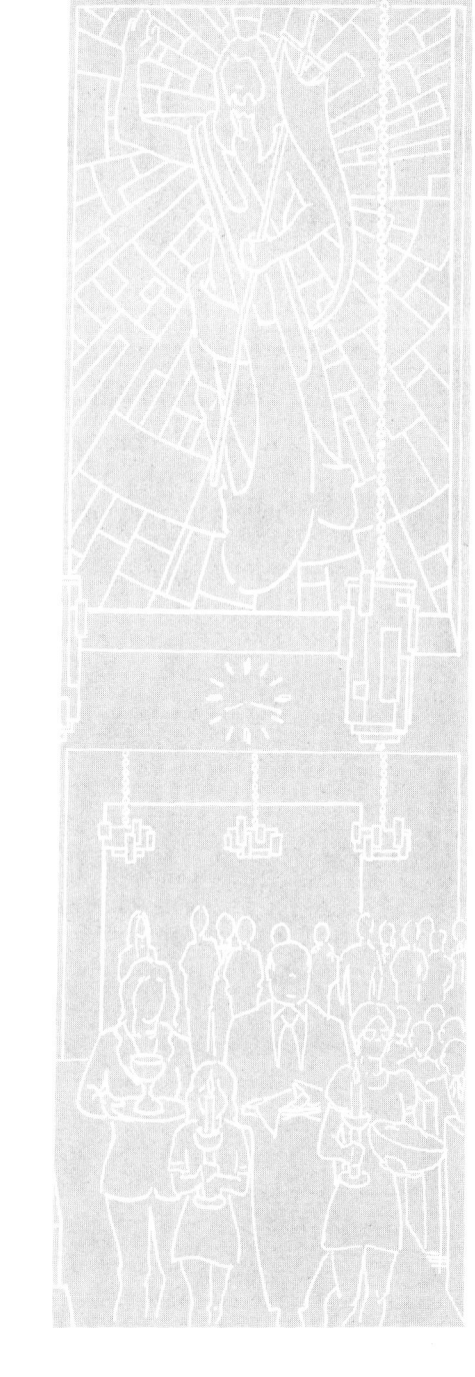

Contents

Foreword / 9
Introduction: Models of the Church and Parish / 13

Section I: Leading and Organizing the Parish

Chapter 1. Leaders of the People
    A Way to Begin / 20
    Listening / 21
    Principles and Priorities / 24
    Getting the People Involved / 27
    Planning Liturgies / 31
    Building a Parish Council / 34
    Leadership Qualities / 36

Chapter 2. A Living Parish
    Prophets and Pastors / 41
    Staff Meetings / 43
    How to Have a Good Meeting / 45
    Starting a Christian Community / 48
    Building a Christian Community / 50
    Various Creative Approaches / 52

Section II: A Believing, Praying, Caring People

Chapter 3. A Praying and Growing People
    Preparing for First Communion / 58
    Eucharistic Prayers for Children / 62
    Eucharistic Prayers for Masses of Reconciliation / 64
    Private and Public Eucharistic Worship / 67
    Whatever Happened to Benediction? / 69

Chapter 4. A Reconciled People
    Sacrament of Reconciliation / 72
    Finding Sins to Confess / 74
    Sensitivity to Sin / 75
    Remodeled Confessionals / 77
    Longer but Better Confessions / 80

    Fears and Tears / 83
    Communal Penance Services / 85
    Expectations of a Confessor / 87
    Three Common Questions About Reconciliation / 90

Chapter 5. A Loving People
    Symbol of the Wedding Ring / 93
    Marriage Encounter / 95
    One-to-One Pre-Cana / 97
    A Policy for Early Marriages / 99
    One-Parent Family Council / 101

Chapter 6. A Believing and Teaching People
    Teachable Moments / 105
    To Teach as Jesus Did / 107
    A Basic Beliefs Course / 109
    Parish Personal Enrichment Week / 111
    Handing Down Our Heritage / 114
    Priests' Pursuit of Wisdom / 116

Chapter 7. A Caring People
    The Mind, Yes; the Heart, No / 119
    By a Dying Person's Bedside / 121
    Discovering an Old Man's Life / 123
    Preparing for the Risen Lord / 125
    Stages of Dying / 128

Section III. The Larger Church and a Wider Vision

Chapter 8. The Bishop: A Leader of Many
    Bishop Topel Speaks on Penance / 134
    Death Comes for the Archbishop / 136
    A Bishop Who Loves His People / 138
    The Bishop as Leader / 140
    Selecting a New Bishop / 142

Chapter 9. Vision of the Future
    Pope John's Dream Coming True:
        The Dawn of a Golden Age / 145
    The Church and the Parish in 1987 / 149

Foreword

On May 1, 1971, I became pastor of Holy Family Church in the upstate New York city of Fulton, New York. After a dozen years as assistant priest in the large, inner-city Syracuse Cathedral and three years as associate director in the Washington office of the Liturgy Secretariat for the National Conference of Catholic Bishops, I finally reached a parish priest's cherished goal: shepherd of one's own flock.

From my experience over those 15 years of pastoral ministry, out of personal observations around the country and through readings on the subject, I had gathered many ideas and principles for developing a living parish.

With the excellent assistance of my priest partners, first Father William Mesmer, then Father Robert Tierney and, finally, Father David Baehr, we began to implement them on a gradual basis. Most of the theories, I am happy to say, worked out very well in practice; some did not and either were modified or discarded.

Our staff grew almost instantly with the addition in September of Mr. (now Father) Ted Auble as religious education coordinator. After his return the following year to the seminary, the parish was fortunate to obtain the services of several Sisters of St. Joseph of Carondolet. They continue to labor today as parish helpers in many areas of concern, including the catechetical instruction field.

During the past five years, several priests have asked me to write down some of the general approaches and practical steps we have followed at Holy Family. This book, basically a compilation of selected and edited columns from the NC News Service "Know Your Faith" series, is a response to those requests.

The Introduction offers a brief theoretical view of a parish based on Avery Dulles' volume, *Models of the Church*.* As the reader might expect, something of each model can be found at Holy Family, with an emphasis probably on the community, sacrament and herald concepts.

Section I contains the overall principles, initial moves and pragmatic procedures we employed during the first months and years. If a newly appointed pastor or freshly elected parish council asked my advice on what to do as a beginning, I would suggest they read this section to capture our philosophy and experience.

Section II describes, through many illustrations, just what the title indicates: a believing, praying, caring people. Not all the incidents involve Holy Family parishioners and some of the material looks at general programs or explains the revised liturgy. However, it fundamentally is a series of stories about people.

The last section has a few thoughts concerning the office of bishop today and a look at the Church or parish of tomorrow.

After each chapter there are two questions for discussion designed to be used with parish councils, adult education

* Published by Doubleday in 1975.

Foreword 11

groups, clergy gatherings, seminary study sessions and the like.

I offer now my deepest gratitude to the magnificent people of Holy Family whose instant love for me on the first Sunday of May, 1971, was but a foretaste of the overwhelming, tear-bringing affection they bestowed on their pastor when he left his flock for a year on that September Sunday, 1976.

I also would like to thank the editors at Ave Maria Press who selected, combined and edited the columns which appear here, leaving me with the lesser task of finishing the manuscript.

Finally, I extend my appreciation to Miss Patricia Reilly of Fulton, New York, who typed the original columns and Mrs. Jean Germano of Rome, Italy, who typed the corrections and additions.

> Rev. Joseph M. Champlin
> Pastor-in-residence, 1976-1977
> North American College
> Rome, Italy

Introduction: Models of the Church and Parish

When a new pastor arrives on the scene, or a fresh parish administration assumes responsibility, both have an excellent, never-to-be-repeated opportunity. They can review in a fresh and thorough way the current condition of the parish, establish certain priorities and agree on long- and short-term desirable goals for the community.

In doing so, these leaders would do well to spend several months listening to comments and suggestions from the people. That input, plus personal observations and other data, will give them a good basis to make some decisions about future trends and practical projects.

However, these people also need to ask themselves a few speculative questions. Where are we as a congregation? What kind of parish should we become? How do we reach that ideal?

The Vatican II Fathers believed that the parish is a little diocese, just as the diocese is a miniature of the universal Church.

In the *Decree on the Apostolate of Lay People* the laity are encouraged continuously "to cultivate the 'feeling for the diocese,' of which the parish is a kind of cell" (No. 10).

The *Liturgy Constitution* also notes: "But as it is impossible for the bishop always and everywhere to preside over the whole flock in his church, he must of necessity establish groupings of the faithful; and, among these, parishes, set up locally under a pastor who takes the place of the bishop, are the most important, for in some way they represent the visible Church constituted throughout the world" (No. 42).

Our understanding of the Church, then, will color our concept of the diocese which, in turn, affects our approach to the parish.

The Church, in the words of scripture, is a mystery. A parish or worshiping community, existing as a miniature of the universal Church, thus shares in that mystical quality. We can never adequately describe or fully understand either.

Our Lord used many illustrations or images to communicate this concept of the Church to his listeners and, ultimately, to us. We think immediately of such familiar expressions as the vine and the branches or the shepherd with his flock of sheep. One theologian listed 96 similar images which can be found in the New Testament.

Father Avery Dulles' classic, *Models of the Church,* can be most helpful in this regard. His analysis of five different models gives individuals in leadership roles a framework within which to analyze those "where, what and how" inquiries.

Something of each model should be found in every parish, but the emphasis on this or that model will vary depending on the circumstances.

For example, an inner-city parish may concentrate on the herald and servant models—preaching to the unchurched and alleviating neighborhood poverty. A mobile suburban congregation, on the contrary, could stress the community and sacrament models—quickly welcoming newcomers and developing effective parent programs preparing youngsters for their first sacramental experiences.

We should note also, however, that no model of the Church should be exaggerated, just as none ought to be omitted. The latter gives an inadequate notion of the Church or parish; the former presents a distorted picture of them.

Moreover, since, as we mentioned, the Church and the parish have a mystical quality to them, these five models do not exhaust their meaning or nature. Additional ones can always be developed. For that reason, all of us need to possess an openness in this area, a flexible attitude ready to expand our vision of the Church and parish.

What follows are brief statements of the parish viewed according to the five models theory of Father Dulles. Accompanying each description are some practical consequences of that concept in parish life and several probing questions to help promote discussion.

Institution. Leaders according to this concept would seek to foster in parishioners a sense of tradition, order, loyalty to the Holy Father and closeness to the bishop. Sending designated persons to the Chrism Mass so they can pick up the holy sacramental oils is one technique which will underscore the unity between parish and bishop. It also illustrates a congregation's oneness through him with the universal Church.

Do you see the Church as an Institution? Does your first thought about the parish turn to the physical plant, the church building, the rectory, the school, the convent? Is your initial impulse to identify Church with priests, bishops, pope? Would you see the parish's primary interest centering around rules to be observed, beliefs to be professed and worship services to be attended?

Community. An administration fostering this model works to build a family or community spirit within the parish, to show each member how they form part of an intimately linked spiritual body. "I am the vine, you are the branches."

Occasional introductions at Sunday liturgies, coffee hours after Mass and name tags during study sessions are a few steps which have proven helpful in this process.

Do you see the Church as a Mystical Community? Is the main effort in your parish to develop community? Are parishioners aware that, as the People of God and members of Christ's Mystical Body, they form a unique communion? Do they see themselves fundamentally as persons linked by an inner, invisible bond, but one expressed in an external way by worship, a profession of faith and special fellowship?

Sacrament. This model believes that the Risen Christ is present in our midst through signs and symbols. The Church thus becomes the visible sign of Jesus' invisible presence.

Attractive vestments, gestures made carefully, baptismal candles and contemporary reconciliation rooms are obvious consequences of this concept which sees Church as sacrament.

Do you see it as a sacrament? Are you conscious that the parish is a sign, a symbol of Jesus' presence in our midst? Is it clear that this external sacrament or sign of an invisible reality can always be improved, and constantly needs to be renewed, reformed and updated? Would you say that the parish's main thrust involves the Sunday Eucharist and the liturgical celebrations for such events as Baptism, Marriage and Christian Burial?

Herald. A biblical, scriptural, gospel preaching and teaching Church—those are notions we embrace according to the herald model.

Parish leaders who try to fulfill this ideal will encourage well-prepared homilies, comprehensive religious education programs for young and old, and bible-oriented prayer groups.

Do you see the Church as a herald? Is your parish's great concern the proclamation of God's word to men? Would you say preaching during the liturgy and religious education programs outside of worship are given the highest priorities with regard to budget, personnel and time?

Servant. This model considers the Church as a group of people reaching out, trying to make the world a better place in which to live, working to overcome today's injustice and misery.

A Thanksgiving Day Mass with food for the poor and a committee for the missions are two possibilities which flow from the servant Church model.

Do you see the Church as a servant? Is it the task of the parish to make the world a better place in which to live? Are activities which occur during the week and outside church the really important work of your worshiping community? Is loving others the entire Christian message? How critical to the nature of your parish and community is the support of boycotts, homilies on world hunger and a program for the elderly?

QUESTIONS FOR DISCUSSION

1. Return to the description of the five models for the Church or parish. Have a member of the group read the material under one model, pause for a period of silent, prayerful reflection, then invite each person to offer his or her comments. After everyone has had an opportunity to speak, move to the next model, then to the third, etc.
2. Having completed this reflection, ask the participants which model or models seem to dominate this particular parish. Should there be a change? What practical steps would that require?

SECTION I

LEADING AND ORGANIZING THE PARISH

1 Leaders of the People

A Way to Begin

Despite the greater involvement of lay people in parish life and the growth of parish councils, a priest still remains today the person in fact most responsible for the vitality of any parish.

Show me the shepherd and I will show you the sheep. He establishes a tone, gives inspiration and provides the direction.

Here are some beginning leadership hints for a recently appointed pastor or a just transferred associate.

Start slowly. While a friend of mine began his pastorate by an "Our world is moving too fast, we can't wait" approach and escaped without major hostility, I think he is an exception which proves the rule.

Normally, parishioners resist change and inwardly resent different approaches unless they clearly meet existing wants or obviously correct poor situations.

Consequently, I recommend initiating no major innovations for six months. Don't be so threatened by your predecessor and so unsure of yourself that you immediately cancel all his programs and begin your own projects.

Praise the man before you, yet make no apologies for yourself.

Meet your people. The shepherd needs to know his sheep, the teacher, the students, the priest, his parishioners.

Pausing in vestments at the main entrance after celebrating Mass and greeting parishioners is one way of meeting your people. Moving around the sparsely populated church before the 7:00 Eucharist and saying "hello" to each of the 68 worshipers is another. Standing outside prior to and following the liturgy when not the celebrant, a third.

A name is the most important word in the human language. Learning it as fast and as well as you can should be high on the priority list of things to do.

Flipping through the emptied, discarded mail-it-monthly offering envelopes will fix names and addresses in a marvelous living computer, your human memory. Those facts, lightly embedded into the mind by a cursory glance, will come back with remarkable frequency when, later, you talk in person to the individual who owns that name and dwells in that house.

A home-visiting parish census, begun immediately and continued consistently, will bear rich spiritual results and obviously widen your knowledge of the people for whom you are responsible.

Win them over. First impressions are important. Therefore, smile, be friendly, show your love. Talk about how glad you are to be here, not how sad you feel leaving there.

Praise them for the good you see; overlook for the present what eventually must be corrected.

Be swift to serve the sick and quick to befriend the young.

Having walked into their homes and won over their hearts, then you can lead them along the pilgrim way to our Father.

Listening

Several decades ago the Catholic Action movement stressed three words as guidelines for apostolic groups: observe, judge, act.

The new priest in a church, or the parish council starting

from scratch, would do well to follow that same process, particularly the initial step.

Those first weeks and months of any administration present golden opportunities to observe (I prefer the term listen). Those in leadership roles have presumably made no major decisions and thus need not feel threatened by criticism of existing programs. Nor does this listening effort necessarily bind the leader(s) into a particular course of action.

In effect, the listeners are saying: "Every person in this parish is important and has the right to be heard. We want to listen, to receive your recommendations. How can we best serve you? What suggestions do you have for us? We may not be able to implement every proposal you make, but at least those points will be noted and given serious consideration."

Small group listening sessions have proven a successful vehicle for this type of consultation in several parishes, in one diocese I know of and in a community hospital.

On the parish level, for example, the recently appointed pastor arranges with the help of established church members a series of neighborhood gatherings in homes. The host and hostess are asked to assemble 10-20 adults on the given evening. Bulletin announcements extend a general welcome to all, with dates and places indicated so no one uninvited feels excluded.

The priest arrives around 8:00 p.m. and is introduced to the individuals present, all of whom wear name tags. He then sits down and, moving around the circle, notes each person's name, address, phone number and occupation. Later, he may snap photographs of the group.

This introductory procedure takes about 15 minutes. It breaks the ice, helps the priest obtain a better grasp of the individual's name and background, usually brings several laughs, promotes a community spirit and facilitates more honest remarks from the participants.

Then by a few words similar to those mentioned above and with pad in hand, he encourages comments or suggestions Some hesitation usually follows, but within a short period first one, next another and another and another will offer observations.

The priest's function here is to listen intently, to jot down salient points and to guide a stalled discussion toward a new area. He should not express agreement or disapproval nor promise action unless in rare cases the proposed matter is an obvious improvement, easily achieved and clearly something which would draw unanimous support.

During the hour and a half, the priest will find he obtains 10-30 suggestions. Some recommendations ("I want more Latin Masses") may be canceled out by the group's own interaction ("We prefer English"); others will be reinforced or weakened by suggestions from later listening sessions.

However, after a few months of repeated home meetings like these in different sections of the parish he will have met 300 to 400 persons, caught some of the prevailing attitudes and received a host of practical proposals.

With that data as background augmented by other personal observations and professional input, he can proceed to project some short- and long-range plans.

The annual report is an excellent medium for summarizing all the suggestions offered through those listening sessions.

Moreover, that published document can include a listing of what was accomplished in the past year as a result of those recommendations ("sidewalk constructed to parking lot, religious education coordinator hired, program of gift-bearers inaugurated").

Finally, it may contain a series of proposed future achievements ("organization of a welcome committee, development of nursery program, new entrance to sacristy").

The Vatican II *Decree on the Ministry and Life of Priests* directed that priests "should be willing to listen to lay people, give brotherly consideration to their wishes, and recognize their experience and competence in the different fields of human activity" (No. 9).

That theoretical advice bears fruit in practice. Parishioners with leaders who listen feel closer to their church, will see personal ideas actually implemented and will be more disposed in the future to volunteer their opinions and energies for the parish.

Principles and Priorities

I suppose there are two basic ways of taking a trip during vacation times. The commercial guided-tour version has everything planned out in precise detail. A more personal approach simply follows today's whims, leisurely moving here or there according to the current desire with only ultimate time and money considerations restricting the itinerary.

The proposed spiritual journey planned by a new pastor or parish administration probably should follow a map which takes a middle course between the fixed guided-tour version and the freewheeling personal approach. There ought to be some fundamental principles giving an overall thrust, but the leaders also need to possess a flexible attitude able to adjust programs as data and circumstances dictate.

The statements which follow were theoretical motions in my mind when I first came to Holy Family. They served as a basis for establishing specific programs and for determining time, personnel and financial priorities. Now, over five years later, I am convinced through experience of their practical soundness.

"Sunday worship is or should be the center of all parish life."

Vatican II's *Liturgy Constitution* gives good support for this principle. ". . . the liturgy is the summit toward which the activity of the Church is directed; it is also the fount from which all her power flows" (Art. 10).

"The Lord's Day is the original feast day, and it should be proposed to the faithful and taught to them so that it may become in fact a day of joy and of freedom from work. Other celebrations, unless they be truly of the greatest importance, shall not have precedence over Sunday, which is the foundation and kernel of the whole liturgical year" (Art. 106).

Some pragmatic consequences of that statement include money for a good music program, ample hours for preaching preparation and careful training of ministers for worship, such as lectors, ushers and servers.

"Parishioners are especially open to and in need of God, the Church, and the priest's presence at the major, or critical moments of their lives."

Those are occasions of birth, growth, love, guilt, sickness, failure, success, death and other situations which touch them deeply inside.

Just this week I rushed to the hospital for prayer over a young man killed in an industrial accident, broke the bad news to stunned parents, held in my arms for a few minutes the boy's sister, comforted his sobbing widow married but a year earlier and informed the elderly grandparents. A draining experience indeed, but a task and a presence both needed and greatly appreciated.

"Preaching God's word requires quality religious education programs."

The new administration must quickly and thoroughly

examine the Catholic school situation, the religious instruction courses for public school students, the sacramental preparation program and the adult religious education possibilities.

That can be an extremely delicate matter, especially in parishes with students split between Catholic and public schools and parents not accustomed to preparing their own children for First Eucharist and Penance or Confirmation.

"Seek maximum participation of persons in the life and activities of the parish."

The freshly appointed leader(s) should make this principle known and clear to all. They will then understand why the new pastor attempts to retain that cluster of persons who have always done everything in the church, yet always seeks to broaden the base and involve more and new individuals in various ways.

"Parishioners will respond generously if money talk is low key, soft sell, spiritual and seldom."

That approach involved significant trust on our part. It was well rewarded. The church debt has been reduced by $70,000 while several substantial capital improvements were made, bills generally paid on time, staff and programs increased.

"The parish must grow in awareness of its social action responsibilities."

Reverent, faith-filled humanly attractive liturgies will supply the inspiration and power. The leaders must then conceive and encourage projects which harness that energy and provide parishioners with opportunities to reach out toward the local, diocesan, national and worldwide needy.

Getting the People Involved

Every person who works actively in a parish or worshiping community for any length of time will taste, sooner or later, bitter disappointment when people do not respond to projects and programs.

It may be the lack of interest in a parish council election, the no-show volunteers for a dance cleanup, the scarcity of people at a carefully prepared Penance service.

Whatever the occasion, the poor response causes discouragement and tempts one to give up.

However, there is no sure guarantee of success for every effort within any community, or in life for that matter. Failures will always occur. The way to cope with those obstacles rests, it seems to me, in a philosophy of acceptance, an ability to move on and, above all, a recognition of the diversity in attitudes among parishioners.

Some people by temperament respond always and to every suggestion with enthusiasm, caution, skepticism, inertia, or hostility.

Other persons react positively or negatively depending on what is proposed. A faithful bingo worker may never consent to serve as a lector at Mass; a reliable special minister for Communion might find parish council deliberations difficult for his or her temperament; a woman who gladly bakes for the parish bazaar may manifest little interest in an adult education series and never agree to teach a CCD class.

Such a variance of attitudes also holds true, unfortunately, with regard to the essential life of a parish—Sunday Eucharists and the grace-giving sacramental liturgies.

There are those who never miss a Sunday, some who come occasionally, others whom we term Christmas and Easter Catholics, and, finally, the "hatched, matched and dispatched" individuals who approach church only for Baptism, Marriage, and funerals.

Accepting these painful realities and making the best of them entails a few practical steps:

- Recognizing that Jesus faced similar situations and spoke about them.
- One of his closest followers betrayed the Lord; another denied knowing him; the rest ran away in his hour of need. Many, even most of those who listened to Christ, rejected his teachings. Furthermore, he predicted his kingdom, his Church would indeed contain a mix of saints and sinners, yet advocated patience lest flickering flames weak in faith be snuffed out instead of kept alive by delicate, long-suffering care.
- Involving individuals in parish life to the extent of their capacity and willingness.

  It is no small contribution for a senior citizen to sew baptismal garments or a family to bring up the gifts or a factory worker to usher week after week.

  Such efforts give these persons a sense of belonging and participation just as lectors, parish council members and singers feel they belong and participate because of their activities.
- Seeking out the stray sheep with loving, gentle determination.

  We spend much of our time in "remedial" spiritual work, calling upon parents who don't care, helping neglected children, healing wounds inflicted long ago. These labors do not always produce results, but the shepherding is God's work and a Christian's obligation.
- Cultivating limited expectations.

  This may sound cynical and opposed to enthusiasm in any endeavor. Not really. It simply means that we recognize the human condition, the probability of occasional failures, and the certainty that we seldom, if ever, will enjoy a total positive response to our efforts.

The leaders, however, should have maximum lay participation as an ideal for the parish. That goal would envision each person engaged in at least one activity of the community.

Here are some pragmatic tips to achieve this end:

- *"Enlist the new, yet retain the old."*

Normally in a parish a relatively small cluster of extremely loyal and generous persons have cared for most of the ongoing tasks. They also are ordinarily the individuals who volunteer for a new project.

The fresh administration must avoid alienating these hardworking people (sometimes long-suffering and little appreciated, too); at the same time, to let them dominate or monopolize every program will stifle growth in others, diminish their enthusiasm and obviously restrict involvement.

Need I mention that the wisdom of Solomon and the sensitivity of a counselor may be required to achieve these desired points?

- *"Specify terms for volunteer service."*

A survey somewhere indicated that volunteers grow weary of the same kind of service after three years. They are not tired of serving; they simply require a new challenge or a different position.

Moreover, people seem to offer talents and energies more freely as well as use them more industriously, if they understand their volunteer efforts are only for a specific period of time. Open-ended volunteerism will succeed, but not so well, nor so happily.

- *"Rotate chairpersons and committee heads."*

For annual parish functions—e.g., dance, picnic, bazaar —and standing committees—e.g., altar rosary, lectors, ushers, the ideal is to have a vice-president or vice-chairperson who understands that he or she will assume the top position during the next year or term. That assures a continuity and eliminates considerable confusion and needlessly expended energies.

- *"Acknowledge services rendered."*

We all like to be recognized, even though our motivation should be for the Lord, the parish, others. A year-end recognition dinner is an obvious method of achieving this, but care ought to be exercised lest some are omitted and odious comparisons made. Bulletin mention has worked similarly and satisfactorily (but with the same risks) for us.

- *"Celebrate volunteer Sunday each fall."*

Next to personal solicitation of volunteers, we have discovered Sunday liturgies and homily time as the most effective manner of recruiting new workers and talents.

Throughout the summer planning period, staff persons should be drawing up a list of possible activities for all age groups. Mimeographed copies of the finished form with pencils are then placed in the pews on the designated Sunday. The theme for that celebration revolves around some aspect of service for the parish community. At homily time, the preacher, after speaking briefly on the topic, invites worshipers to take volunteer sheets, mark at least one area, and drop in the collection basket. These volunteer sheets should ask for name, address, phone number and Mass regularly attended.

A note on the ones we used stated: "If already involved in the activity at Holy Family, please do NOT check the space."

Below this directive were 37 possibilities for service and a final one, number 38: "Other —, please specify."

We attempted to offer an opportunity for persons of every age. The form thus suggested the following: altar server (must be at least grade 4), high school youth group, college winter and summer get-together, golden age club (must be over 50).

It also included tasks suited to nearly every temperament and talent. The list began with bingo worker, touched giftbearer at Sunday Mass, altar bread baker, Welcome to Holy Family committee, parish press operator and concluded with Fulton Catholic School helper.

The response? We received over 250 forms, with the vast majority checking several positions. Moreover, these volunteers were almost entirely fresh recruits since veteran workers already in a program did not sign for that activity—we already had their names.

Now, instead of six bakers we had 15; rather than seven artists for the musical leaflet we could call on 12; to our rotating list of 175 Sunday Mass gift-bearers, we added 25 names.

We picked up 250 new volunteers. The staff, however, must be certain to contact each person sometime during the coming 12 months for a volunteer task. Otherwise, the individual who offered his or her talent and time will very likely feel resentment and refuse to cooperate in the next year's program.

Planning Liturgies

In another city recently I participated in a very solemn Mass for a special commemorative occasion.

The music was superlative—a large choir (imagine having 30 men singers in your parish group), a talented and energetic director, a fine pipe organ, an assortment of other instrumentalists. I am not sure, however, the people worshiped superlatively.

Their speaking and singing parts seemed minimal; the

distractions and activity around the altar were frequent and pronounced. The congregation watched, listened, enjoyed and perhaps drew considerable inspiration from the liturgy. For the most part, nevertheless, they were mute spectators, a role rejected years ago by several papal documents.

With minimal direction, that Eucharistic celebration could easily have fused this marvelous choral music and the people's proper parts. The congregation's share would then be enhanced without any diminution of the choir's important function.

Careful, informed advance planning remains the key to such a delicate fusion, just as similar early preparation is essential for effective regular Sunday worship. This presumes, of course, that parish leaders establish weekend liturgies on the highest rung of their priority ladder. Such a value judgment will have practical consequences with regard to time, money, personnel and energy expenditures.

For us, Sunday liturgy planning begins a month or two earlier at special staff meetings. We seek to develop themes for the next four to eight weekend celebrations (e.g., all of Advent, Lent, Eastertime or a section of the ordinary time throughout the year). Those sessions are hardworking, painful, yet creative and crucial for the development of celebrations which can touch the hearts of parishioners.

Having studied the scriptural texts for those Sundays, reflected on the current needs of the community and discussed at length possible ideas, we finally agree on subjects or topics and preachers for each weekend.

That list then goes to two groups: our musicians and artists.

An ever-changing committee of the choir takes the themes and selects music—some familiar, some new—which will underscore aspects of those various topics. Each artist receives the subject for a given Sunday and starts to prepare a cover for that weekend's song leaflet.

Since the theme for the coming homily and liturgy is known, the previous week's bulletin indicates, to illustrate, "Next Sunday, Father Baehr will preach on God's power and desire to heal us."

The preacher, aware early of the date and topic, can thus read around the subject and prayerfully reflect over a period of days or weeks on the theme. Moreover, he may also enlist the aid of a committee, a few individuals, or a family for ideas and suggestions.

On the day or two prior to his preaching date, the priest or deacon then completes the homily in detail, prepares the general intercessions and introductory scriptural comments, selects the most appropriate options from the sacramentary, and writes a few remarks for the celebrant, particularly a mini-homily after Communion.

This process takes me approximately five hours. That effort, however, has been rewarded many times over by the obvious impact which some of our better liturgies exert on worshipers.

Weekend Masses are the occasions when most or at least the greatest number of parishioners come together for listening and prayer. The major moments of life—birth, growth, guilt, sickness, love, death and crises—are those events when these same people are most disposed to listen and pray.

Parish leaders, conscious of this, should free priests of administrative labors so they can spend the time needed with persons experiencing such situations. The clergy naturally need to recognize the sensitivity of those occasions and give themselves in the service of those particularly happy or hurting.

For example, accompanying a terminally ill person and his or her family through dying and death requires, ideally, more than one visit to the hospital for the Sacrament of Anointing the Sick. More may not be demanded, but more really is expected and more will never be forgotten.

Building a Parish Council

In a parish where Vatican II-oriented leadership has never existed or been lacking for a lengthy period of time, I am not sure establishment of the parish council would be first on my priority list of objectives.

This is neither a denial of the council's importance nor a wish to reserve jealously all decision-making for the clergy.

On the contrary, councils are essential for the full and active involvement of lay persons in the life of any parish. Moreover, council members need to see that their opinions have impact and understand that their words reach ears willing to listen.

Nevertheless, parishioners in a church with behind-the-times liturgies and little or no adult religious education programs are, in most cases, not well equipped to make informed judgments about certain aspects of parish life.

For example, the sign of peace, Communion received standing, more substantial altar breads, programs in which parents prepare children for first reception of sacraments and the conversion of confessionals into reconciliation rooms are items which would run into heavy opposition from many parish council members unaware of the reasons behind such moves. Their gut reactions and emotional resistance would tend to doom them from the start.

In this type of parish, admittedly an exception today, I would thus first initiate a gradual program of updating the liturgy in accord with papal directives and of improving religious education in line with approved diocesan regulations.

Then, a year or so later, we could begin the process of forming a parish council.

A search or steering committee composed of representative parishioners would make the preliminary steps. This group should read some of the pertinent literature (John XXIII Publications has a variety available), visit neighboring parishes to observe councils in action, and obtain sample by-laws and constitutions.

With that as background, the steering unit would organize an educational program for the parish at large. Homilies, handouts and bulletin messages are the easiest methods for mass communication; small group discussions require more effort, but probably exert a deeper influence.

The final task for this steering group is to suggest a tentative organization of the council and to conduct an election.

At Holy Family we were anxious to have more elected representatives than *ex officio* or appointed ones. Consequently, the council is small (five parish staff persons and six elected laity). The election, despite good education and publicity plus an attractive ballot with photos of candidates, proved disappointing. We experienced difficulty securing candidates and less than 50 percent of the parishioners voted.

Once under way it was made clear to council members that the major decisions for the parish were, ideally, to pass from the staff (aided by the two trustees in exceptional cases) to them. At the same time, they understood the pastor ultimately possessed a veto power, if a decision ran contrary to diocesan church policy.

In some ways, the occasionally bitter debate about a council's decision-making or consultative-only function appears to me a bit academic. A council wields great power—moral, persuasive power, even if its role has been clearly defined as advisory.

A pastor with any degree of sensitivity to his leadership position in contemporary society should move only most reluctantly in a direction clearly opposed by a majority of the council. In theory I believe he could and should, but those would be rare instances.

On the other hand, the pastor (or parish team) which frequently ignores a council's recommendation will soon have discontented representatives and a terminally ill unit.

Here are a few practical tips for the successful operation of an established parish council.

• Some time at each meeting should be allocated for the members' intellectual and spiritual growth. Prayer and scripture, a filmstrip, book review or presentation come readily to mind for this. An annual Mass would also be highly desirable.

• The president should prepare a careful and detailed agenda in advance. One cannot run a smooth meeting without such preliminary efforts.

• The president must seek to combine a strong leadership function which keeps the group on target with a great concern that each representative enjoy the freedom to speak when so moved.

• Committees ought to be functional or be disbanded.

• Occasional socializing (e.g., a dinner, wine and cheese after a meeting) helps build a better working relationship among council members.

Leadership Qualities

I wish to outline several qualities which, in my view, parish leaders should possess. They apply, in varying degrees and differing ways, of course, to several persons and groups who exercise leadership roles in the worshiping community.

Thus, for example, we can speak about these characteristics in a pastor, his associate, the religious education coordinator, members of the parish council and the liturgical committee, the president of an organization like the Men's Guild or the Altar-Rosary Society, teachers in the Catholic school or in the CCD program.

Those qualities (and this is not an exhaustive list) are:

VISION. Leaders must have a picture of the future, a glimpse of what ought to be, what can be.

Jesus serves as the perfect model, both as a visionary, and as a leader possessing the characteristics which will follow. He spoke to people about his Father's house in which there are many mansions; he pictured for his listeners a kingdom yet to come, one which they must help build; he set goals, elusive ideals for his followers which never can be completely attained and therefore will always demand renewed efforts to achieve them, a constant starting over, reaching out, striving to become the kind of individual which I am not now, but should be and, with God's grace, could be.

Parish leaders obviously need to pattern their efforts after Christ's example. His task is our task; his message, ours; his vision, our vision.

COURAGE. This quality flows as a necessary consequence from the preceding one. Most people, perhaps all persons to some degree and in certain areas, do not enjoy taking a risk and leaving what is secure. Only reluctantly do we launch out into the deep or walk where the water is over our heads. Comfortable with what we have, sure of the present ground, we tend to fear the unknown and with reluctance follow a strange path.

A visionary must lead followers into all those areas—away from the secure, into the risky, over their heads, into the deep, along strange paths and into the beyond, the unknown.

Once all have arrived at the higher level, the better state, and are acclimated to their new surroundings, the fears and the discomforts normally pass. These people feel pleased with the progress made and rejoice over their new homes.

Followers often do not want to go where the leader is taking them and grumble, resist, resent the move. Yet, after the journey is finished, they see the wisdom behind the step and curiously enough tend to praise themselves for the vision and forget the one who brought them there.

Courage to overcome those objections in the beginning and patience when critics conveniently forget their earlier hostility or reluctance after the promised land is reached are essential ingredients for a good leader.

This, I know, is rather abstract and philosophical. But those who were instrumental in the introduction of a vernacular liturgy, or of altars facing the people, or of lay ministers for Holy Communion, or of parental preparation programs for First Eucharist will clearly recognize the patterns described above and understand their practical application in parish life.

SCIENTIFIC SENSITIVITY. There are obviously two aspects of this particular attribute. First, it demands on the part of the leader a certain openness to the feelings of those under his or her direction. Secondly, it presupposes that the way in which one seeks to discover the constituents' attitudes will be orderly, objective and not based on hearsay, surface impressions or the articulate objections of a vocal minority.

That openness means a willingness to listen and truly to hear what the rank and file are saying. Otherwise the leader soon becomes a dictator, one moving alone and without consultation, bulldozing ahead regardless of reluctance within the general body. In time, that path can only lead to disaster for any leader.

I find most people do not expect leaders always to follow

their suggestions—they know this is not possible from a realistic viewpoint. Nevertheless, these same persons want to be heard, want serious consideration given to their thoughts, their recommendations, their attitudes.

Leaders generally convey such openness in many non-verbal ways. People sense instinctively this person wants to hear what you have to say. That recognition comes out in phrases like: "He really is open" or "You can talk to her" or "They listened to us."

Deft posing of questions helps. The manner in which we make an inquiry often implies the kind of answer we want.

Consider, for example, these three possibilities: "How do you like the changes in the Church since Vatican II?" "What changes in the Church haven't you liked since Vatican II?" "How do you feel about the changes in the Church since Vatican II?" The first two questions are looking for certain types of responses—positive ones, then negative replies. The last welcomes either. The final method will more likely bring an honest expression of opinion.

Anonymity also facilitates the procedure. My public school religious education class students normally will not tell me the year's course was most unsatisfactory either in person or even on a slip of paper, if their names must be appended to it. But give them an anonymous questionnaire, indicate your wish to learn their frank evaluations, and watch out!

A senior pupil wrote that my presentations were "lousy." The worst class was the first one, the best was the last one and the main thing learned throughout the year—how to cope with boredom.

Such sensitivity, however, should also be scientific. Leaders need to distinguish between complaints of the few, especially those who find problems with every development, and the objections of the many, who in effect tell us we moved too fast or in the wrong direction.

Is this criticism the tip of an iceberg or an isolated piece of ice floating down the river? If it is the former, we must adjust our program; if the latter, we listen intently, sympathetically, but cautiously continue forward.

Overall response of the senior class, to illustrate, rated the religion course "terrific" or "good" (24 out of 27), despite the solo "lousy" evaluation noted above.

THICK-SKINNED. Most persons want to be loved by all, enjoy universal approval, gain 100 percent acceptance. Wise leaders know those are but utopian dreams.

If one close follower betrayed Jesus another denied him and the rest ran away at his darkest moment then today's less talented, less holy leader must also expect opposition from many and rejection by some.

Leaders should indeed be sensitive persons, but not too sensitive.

QUESTIONS FOR DISCUSSION

1. Discuss the positive and negative aspects of leaders moving ahead swiftly or taking a gradual approach. Use a few examples from the recent past (e.g., the sign of peace, lay ministers of communion) or the possible future (e.g., married clergy, women priests) to help spark the discussion.
2. Quickly go through the qualities of a leader and describe contemporary persons and local situations which illustrate each.

2 A Living Parish

Prophets and Pastors

Last week I met Father Dan Berrigan twice within the space of 24 hours.

The first encounter came in Boston at Logan Airport as we both boarded an Allegheny plane for our common home base in Upstate New York.

It was certainly a study in contrasts. Dan wore his familiar black beret, desert boots, sport shirt, heavy sweater and slacks with an apparently underground newspaper tucked into a small, battered suitcase. I was dressed in my customary Roman collar, black suit, long-sleeved white shirt and cuff links with the *New York Times* in one hand and a neat, efficient-looking Samsonite attache case in the other.

Those external differences reflected equally divergent inner attitudes and approaches. Dan is today's prophet, a poet, philosopher, master of prose; he speaks sharply, even if beautifully, cuts, pricks our consciences, raises questions, makes us uncomfortable, challenges the status quo, walks alone, infuriates establishment people, leaves one wondering if he is a proud, self-appointed judge and maverick or a humble, unselfish martyr and true follower of Christ.

I see myself, on the other hand, as a cautious conservative in temperament, taste and doctrine, a reconciler, one who seeks to blend the riches of our tradition with the needs of this age, reluctant to speak harshly, anxious to persuade rather than confront, a soft-selling good guy, and one inclined to prefer the established order and the usual way.

Yet we have many mutual acquaintances and shared loves. Dan has, for example, lunched with my film critic brother at the Cannes festival and I knew his brother and sister-in-law fairly well during my days at the Syracuse Cathedral. So, too, our loves for God, for Christ, for the Church, for the priesthood, for persons in spiritual or material need, while expressed in radically different ways, spring, I trust, from a similar source.

My second encounter came that night at home when I picked up the latest issue of *Commonweal* and read Dan's "An Open Letter to Joe O'Rourke" with its somewhat typical Berrigan subtitle: "To hell with the glory of God; or, how we got rid of Joe."

The article, of course, dealt with a fellow Jesuit dismissed from the Society of Jesus for several incidents, the last of which was baptizing a baby in Marlboro, Massachusetts, despite his superior's admonition to the contrary. Readers will probably recall that painful event involving a mother whose stand on an abortion issue caused the local parish priests to refuse Baptism until they had resolved the question with her.

Dan, as I read it, believed O'Rourke was unwise in this case, but praised his other efforts and deplored the dismissal. The essay gave him an opportunity to offer some bitter criticisms of the Jesuits, Church officials, our government and contemporary situations.

I disagreed with some parts of that article, just as I have often found objectionable Dan's thoughts and actions in the past.

But Dan Berrigan is good for me, and persons like him are good for the growth of any parish. He and they shake complacency, stir us to read, think, sometimes to act, and remind Christians that Jesus constantly calls his followers to new, higher goals, to patterns of life which may run contrary to the established, accepted norms of the world around us.

Staff Meetings

I remember that during my first dozen years as a priest at the Cathedral (1956-1968) there was never a staff meeting.

I was working with three other competent, conscientious assistant pastors under an elderly, generally inactive, but wise rector. In that large, downtown, extremely busy church, we had, I thought, a relatively smooth-flowing operation.

Each priest knew his particular areas of responsibility and was left free to direct them according to his own unique talents and tastes. Common "duties" were equally shared on the basis of a long-established, rotating system.

We never prayed together except for grace before and after meals. Nevertheless there were many moments of "togetherness," a term unknown then, but an obvious reality in that unstructured community of Cathedral priests. We talked often about parish life and pastoral problems, but these discussions were during informal moments after dinner, following Saturday night confessions or at the end of the day, sitting in front of a television set.

Neither can I recall a goal-setting session, an agenda, or someone formally chairing the discussion.

Those were different days, however, and what proved satisfactory at the Cathedral then would never suffice today. I was not surprised, therefore, to learn that now the Cathedral priests (and other employees) gather every Friday morning at 9 a.m. for an hour-long staff meeting, with the clergy remaining afterwards for a discussion of matters applicable only to them.

We do not hold staff meetings at Holy Family in Fulton on such a precisely regular basis, but ours are nonetheless frequent, lengthy, essential for the effective functioning of parish life, and a source of hope or encouragement for all concerned.

I offer the following observations as a result of four years' experience with such sessions:

- Staff meetings do not just happen, the parish leader has to make them happen. Unless the time and date are established by a predetermined schedule (like the Cathedral) or by common agreement at the last session (our normal procedure at Holy Family), staff meetings tend to be delayed or never held.

- The leader should prepare an open-ended agenda in advance, ideally with all participants knowing beforehand and contributing topics to his list of topics for discussion.

- Common prayer starts the meeting in the right direction and with a proper spirit. Midday prayer from the Liturgy of the Hours, for example, serves this purpose well.

- A different dynamic governs staff discussions. For the leader to consult each person individually is not identical to a group discussion of the same subject. During my first year as a pastor I did much of the former; in the ensuing years I realized my mistake and shifted to the more difficult, but more satisfactory, staff system.

- Staff meetings should deal with both immediate, nitty-gritty details (dates for First Communion meetings, topics for homilies over the next four weeks) and long-range goals and objectives (where will we be five years from now, what programs will be initiated throughout the coming year).

- The summer months provide excellent opportunities for a more relaxed, less pressured planning of the 10 months of activities which begin in September. Once school and religious instruction programs start, time becomes a precious commodity and our efforts generally revolve around the day-to-day operation of projects already under way.

• Participants need to develop an ability to disagree in a helpful, constructive way without becoming personal, hostile or defensive.

• A combination of staff prayer, discussion and socializing is highly desirable. This year we have frequently met from 4:00 to 5:00 p.m., celebrated the 5:15 Mass, then shared refreshments, dinner and even the rest of an evening before burning logs in the fireplace.

How to Have a Good Meeting

American Catholics live in a society now dominated by countless committees and endless meetings.

The Church to which they belong is naturally affected by that environment. We have, as a result, parish councils, liturgy commissions, school boards, committees for dances, committees for bazaars, committees for picnics, committees for retreats, committees for almost everything.

The future for most of us will mean membership in many such groups and attendance at frequent meetings. There are, of course, good and bad meetings, poorly run sessions and highly satisfying ones.

I have found through experience that the following common-sense points, if observed, facilitate productive, orderly meetings and prevent frustrating, pointless sessions.

• Start and be on time. The first is a chairman's responsibility, the second, everyone's duty. Late arrival habits soon are corrected when a leader begins promptly at the appointed hour regardless of who is present.

- Open with prayer and a reading from the bible. Christ is present where two or three gather in his name and through the proclamation of inspired scriptural words. Those reasons alone would justify such steps. However, these prayerful, reflective moments at the outset tend also to remind participants they assemble not as debaters or politicians, but as members of a worshiping community reaching for sacred goals.
- Prepare in advance an agenda with fairly clear time limits both for the total meeting and for specific topics as well.

This procedure requires considerable preparation by the chairperson and staff (if any). Those efforts nevertheless bear immediate rewards by communicating to others of the committee a sense of purpose and direction. Furthermore, it places indirect pressure on all to avoid digressions and to speak with a succinct pointedness.

Agendas, on the other hand, should remain relatively open and a chairperson careful lest the prepared list with its timetable irk members or cause them to feel inhibited. Getting through on schedule is highly desirable, but not an end in itself nor a result to be achieved at any cost.

- Chair the meeting in a firm, yet flexible manner.

The leader here needs tact, wisdom and the Holy Spirit's guidance. He or she must keep participants on the track, stop wandering discussions, shut off the repetitious, the long-winded. At the same time, a chairperson should give each person who so desires a suitable opportunity to speak.

A committee appreciates firmness in a leader who can move them along, separating the essential from the accidental. Members, however, resent a too heavy-handed or dictatorial approach by the chairperson.

For those in leadership roles I recommend a small, practical paperback, *The Person Who Chairs the Meeting* by

A Living Parish

Paul O. Madsen (Judson Press, Valley Forge, Pa. 19481, $1.95).

- As a member, speak when you have something to contribute, but also listen to what others say and don't dominate the discussion.

Some individuals like to hear themselves talk, while others believe, erroneously, they are expected as a member of the committee to comment on every topic.

- Learn to disagree without becoming personal.

Friendships need not suffer (although they often do) because two persons argue strongly on opposite sides of an issue. In such circumstances with particularly delicate and volatile questions, the chairperson sometimes would be wise to ask for a vote by secret ballot. This enables individuals to express their honest opinions without fear of offending one who has heatedly defended the contrary view.

- Quickly assign to subcommittees matters which are highly complex or do not enjoy an immediate consensus from the group. A full board of many members is usually not the place to hammer out details or to work out compromises.

- Stagger and limit terms. Committee personnel generally function more reliably and effectively when they know their obligation to this group is for a specific period of reasonable length. Moreover, fresh faces and ideas always invigorate a deliberating board.

- If you possess neither the time nor the interest to serve as a regular, active participant in the group, either say no when asked in the beginning or resign, if you already are a member.

A few really good members are better than many poor ones.

Starting a Christian Community

Dividing an established, excessively large suburban parish and forming from it a new faith community is not an easy task.

It requires a pastor willing to let go, a shepherd who neither clings to favorite parishioners nor who jealously guards an empire he may have developed.

It also requires a spiritual leader who can start from scratch, tap the available resources and chart an original course of action.

Finally, it requires people who will give their land, their time, their energies, their money to build a new parish complex and more, a new community of believing Christians.

That is the story of Christ the King Church in Liverpool, New York (the established parish) and St. John's in neighboring Clay (the offspring of Christ the King).

Monsignor James McCloskey was the giving, willing shepherd who saw the need of a new parish, negotiated for the land necessary and encouraged from the pulpit his beloved people in the cutoff area to join the new St. John's.

Father James O'Connell was (and is) the spiritual leader who with his incredible energy, hard work and forward-thinking approach forged in but four years the faith community at Clay.

It was, however, in the last analysis, a group of generally young, enthusiastic, middle-class, relatively well-educated, generous, typically mobile suburban persons who, responding to Msgr. McCloskey's recommendation and Father O'Connell's pioneer leadership, fashioned the physical plant and spiritual community which is St. John's.

Father O'Connell first preached at Christ the King announcing establishment of the new parish, with his words strongly supported by the pastor.

A Living Parish

Within a week, he arranged for an interim office and chapel in a recently vacated house and by the end of the month publicized, again through Christ the King's pulpit, a schedule of Sunday Masses at two community locations—the local theater and a municipal auditorium.

That summer, in addition to mailing informational letters to potential parishioners, Father O'Connell held 30 evening meetings at different homes with clusters of three to four couples. He discussed with them their hopes and dreams of what St. John's should be.

The initial decision of these people was to construct immediately a parish administration building which could serve as a combination rectory, temporary chapel and office.

With that attractive house in operation, they turned to the future and clearly indicated their preference for a church which could also be used for other purposes, not a social hall which would double as a church.

A committee composed of the pastor, two trustees and four persons (two men, two women) appointed by the parish council directed the design and construction of this multi-purpose structure. They selected Mr. Jack Teitsch from seven architects who competed for that post. He then executed the plans for a $700,000-plus church (including furniture and costly landscaping) with a seating capacity of 600.

Well designed for visuals and with removable chairs, it has already on several occasions been converted through a minimum of effort into space for community and parish movies, concerts, dinners and dances.

The beginning efforts at St. John's, of necessity, revolved around the organization of people and the development of physical buildings in which parishioners could work, pray and play. But its leaders always kept a clear view of the parish's ultimate purpose. They verbalized this vision in the foreword of a booklet produced for distribution to new and old members.

"St. John's is more than an architecturally unique church located on Soule Road; it is more than a congregation of 900 Catholic families in Northwest Clay; St. John's is much more than a multifunctional building serving parishioners and the community at large. More importantly, St. John's strives to be a loving Christian community working and worshiping God together in the spirit of the gospel and the renewal of Vatican Council II. It is in this mode that all Catholics are invited to participate freely in the activities of St. John's."

Building a Christian Community

Involvement of every parishioner in the life of St. John's parish, Clay, New York, is the goal which the pastor, Father James O'Connell, and the community leaders uphold for its 900 families. They call this attitude or approval "volunteerism" and on Volunteer Sunday each September they distribute forms which afford people an occasion to review their past participation in the church's activities and offer their services for the coming year.

The impact of that philosophy can be seen in the following projects or procedures at St. John's:

• The parish council consists of the clergy, trustees, chairpersons of 10 standing committees, and 10 elected at-large members. Most of the practical discussions are made by the various committees with the council, which meets every other month, normally limiting itself to long-range plans and policies for the parish.

• Upkeep of the facilities is accomplished not by the customary custodian, but through the men's maintenance committee. These men work Saturday mornings according to a rotating schedule approximately every eight weeks from 8:00 a.m. to

10:00 a.m. The money saved as a result of this volunteerism has enabled the parish to hire a full-time music director and liturgist, Miss Phyllis Brandoin.

• Miss Brandoin, who has been trained in organ, piano and guitar, guides the liturgical and paraliturgical programs at St. John's. The published Mass schedule indicates the variety of styles which the staff, under her direction, provides for worshipers.

5:00 p.m. Saturday	— Folk Mass
8:00 a.m. Sunday	— Quiet and Tranquil
10:00 a.m. Sunday	— The Principal Mass — Organ Prelude and Postlude — Congregational singing — Senior choir
12:00 Noon Sunday	— Organ Prelude and Postlude — Congregational singing.

• St. John's has been experimenting recently with a series of monthly communal penance services at different hours. The attendance has been good, ranging from 70 to 300, but they have not determined the optimum hour for that rite or even if there is one.

• This summer the parish conducted a five-day, house-to-house, doorbell-ringing, census-taking apostolate to the 2,400 residences of the area.

Father O'Connell involved 300 persons—two cochairpersons, 10 division or district leaders, 50 team captains and 200 committee members. All of these received census kits and appropriate instructions at a session directed by the pastor and held for their convenience in the morning, afternoon or evening.

Parishioners had been prepared for the visitation by two

explanatory homilies. Others in the community were, I presume, aware of the project through word of mouth and publicity via the local mass media.

The visitors distributed several items at homes with Catholic residents.

—A census form to be filled out, sealed in an envelope and returned to Father O'Connell for opening.

—A flier on the why of Sunday Mass prepared originally in London, Ontario, Canada, and adapted by our own diocesan liturgical commission.

—A booklet outlining the various committees and activities of St. John's.

—A letter from the pastor mentioning the Holy Year of Reconciliation and urging persons who feel alienated from the Church through bad past experiences or by particularly difficult present situations to contact the staff at St. John's for assistance.

The tone of this letter and the approach of the visitors was intended to be warm and positive, encouraging people to become part of the believing, loving Christian community which St. John's is or at least hopes to become.

Various Creative Approaches

The Jesuit fathers who direct and staff St. Ignatius Parish in Mobile, Alabama, use various creative approaches for the spiritual growth of their people and the steady improvement of their worship. Some of these basic concepts could be easily and profitably adapted by many of our Catholic churches in the United States.

Membership and Activities Committee.

When a new parishioner or family enrolls at St. Ignatius,

A Living Parish 53

they promptly receive a letter from the chairperson of this group with several enclosures. That packet includes a directory containing a list of all parish members with a brief description of the church's various organizations, a copy of the weekly bulletin, a time and ability volunteer form, and a flier explaining their tithing program.

Some phrases from the welcoming letter typify the spirit behind this effort:

"A cordial welcome to St. Ignatius Parish! Your fellow parishioners are happy that you have joined us and we hope that you will find spiritual and material benefits in your new residence. . . . May you have many happy years in the parish."

Host and hostess for Mass.

The liturgical committee has developed a corps of persons whose task it is to arrive for Sunday liturgies 15 minutes early.

An explanatory letter to those who accepted this responsibility summarizes their function:

"We firmly believe that your task is one of paramount importance, because true celebration requires a sense of love that others in our parish feel for each one of us. This, in essence, we believe is your role: to show some of the love of others, of Jesus, for each person at our liturgy, by saying 'hello' or 'good morning' or whatever you think appropriate.

"This warm greeting naturally will be extended to your friends, those whom you know by sight, etc., but we especially urge you to greet the stranger, the one whose face is unfamiliar to you, because chances are that he will be unfamiliar to most and therefore might go unacknowledged but for your greeting."

Male and female lectors.

Each weekend Mass has two lectors (a practice some might question, believing a single reader is more effective), one a man, the other a woman.

These pairs were not, at least on the occasion I observed, husband and wife teams (a procedure familiar to and strongly encouraged by Marriage Encounter couples), but simply random combinations of men and women—some married, others not.

Stewardship of time and ability.

New parishioners upon arrival and old members once a year have an opportunity to offer their services for a host of tasks. They do so by means of a sheet which suggests 50 possibilities in the areas of worship, service, Christian formation, parish school, publicity, maintenance and marriage preparation.

The introductory paragraph reads:

"In grateful response to God for his generous gifts of time and ability to me as his steward, I volunteer to return to God, as I am able, my time and ability for Christ's work in my parish as indicated below."

Tithing.

Father Herbert Conner, the pastor, and his staff refined and revitalized a tithing program several years ago in which parishioners were asked to donate five percent of their income to the church. The other five percent of that tithing for God would be given by the member to other charities.

This paragraph from their annual financial report summarizes the spirit behind tithing at St. Ignatius:

"The tithe takes the form of a prayer, an act of worship, to acknowledge his living providence in your life. You give to God also to express your thanks for his many blessings, and God will not be outdone by your generosity. God knows what you really need and he will give it to you in abundance."

The results have, I think, been remarkable. In a parish of 750 registered families the receipts for 1974-75 came to

A Living Parish

$283,955. This enabled the parish last year to pay off $100,000 of the debt and still subsidize the school operation to the tune of $55,000.

Father Conner is convinced of the blessings this generosity brings upon the givers. He writes: "During the days ahead, you and your loved ones will surely experience joys from God. A thousand joys. Too rich to measure. Too beautiful to describe."

QUESTIONS FOR DISCUSSION

1. Describe some good and some poor meetings you have attended recently, some good and some poor chairpersons (without naming names). Why were they good? Why were they poor?
2. Discuss the pros and cons of asking parishioners to tithe. Do the same with regard to the Sunday collection, that is, giving 10 percent of it to the needy on the local, national and international levels by, for example, adopting a dozen poor parishes around the world.

SECTION II

A BELIEVING, PRAYING, CARING PEOPLE

3 A Praying and Growing People

Preparing for First Communion

Last month we completed our fourth parental preparation program for First Holy Communion. The sister in charge and all of us who participated in it agree that through this four-year experience—a period mixed with many mistakes and deep disappointments as well as positive results and inspirational events—we have finally developed a reasonably successful system.

In brief, the program opens with a two-hour general meeting for all the parents in October, continues with one small group session in homes throughout November and concludes by a real, but demonstration and teaching Mass, also in homes, during December.

One of the contemporary commercial texts is used for both parent and child. Once a youngster has finished the book and the parents judge that the child is ready for the Eucharist, they arrange an interview with me or my partner priest at Holy Family. The boy or girl then receives our Lord for the first time with the family (about 75 percent select that option) or waits until our Solemn Parish First Communion Celebration at a Sunday Mass in May. All the youngsters, even those who have already communicated earlier with the family, are invited to participate in this spring ceremony.

We certainly will find ways in the future to improve aspects of this procedure. However, we did learn much in the process of polishing the program. Following are some general conclusions or observations about these parental preparation efforts:

• First Communion time is a potent teachable moment for parents. As Sister and I drove home on those cold, snowy December nights after our concluding home Masses, we reiterated every evening just how effective the program seems to be.

Parents who begin in October with hesitation or even hostility slowly come to see its value and by the pre-Christmas Eucharistic celebrations normally are quite enthused. They find it draws them closer to their children; they discover a deepening of their own faith; they smile with surprise at how much their child has learned in a few months of joint home study; they react with amazement at the youngsters' quiet attention throughout this one-hour explanatory Mass.

• Firm insistence on parental participation in the program is critical to its success.

In my optimistic naivete when we first initiated this system, I expected our fathers and mothers would rejoice over the opportunity for such intimate involvement in the religious formation of their children. Then came the folded arms, frowns, silent looks, out-of-hearing negative comments ("That really is the priests' and sisters' job!" or "Why am I sending my children to Catholic school, if we have to do this?").

Some of the opposition developed, of course, from parents who didn't really care or who resented the effort entailed. However, most of the objections arose, I think, from a sense of inadequacy on the part of parents, a lack of confidence in their ability to teach and train their children in this important area.

One needs to be patient during those introductory years, because parents and parishioners require time to accept the concept, and priests and instructors need time to perfect the program.

Sometimes, nevertheless, a softness of approach from parish leaders with regard to the new system can be misinterpreted as the absence of conviction about its value. We followed that path for three years and frequently came home from meetings very discouraged by the poor attendance.

This year the kickoff homily announcing our program took a much firmer stance. We set a definite cutoff date for registration, stressed the importance of parental participation, and indicated that at least one parent was to attend each session.

The response has been gratifying. Negative comments either stopped or went underground. Parents arrived in good numbers for every session with an encouragingly larger number of fathers on hand. The feedback after the final Masses was in most instances very supportive, particularly from parents who initially had serious reservations about the new program.

- A detailed schedule for the entire year with built-in options should be presented to the parents at the opening night.

This requires considerable advance planning by the parish leadership personnel, but it pays handsome dividends in terms of increased parental attendance.

After the initial sign-up for this program, fathers and mothers were offered two nights as alternatives for the opening session. At that first meeting, we gave them informational sheets outlining the dates and places for all the events to follow. Moreover, each family was placed in a particular group with phone numbers and addresses of every host couple listed on the schedule.

Under such an arrangement, the parents are able to plan

ahead and, when conflicts develop, make the necessary adjustments.

We have employed with success a similar system for lectors, gift-bearers, and special ministers of Communion.

• Parents returning for the preparation of other children need to be integrated into the program but with special accommodations based on their previous experience.

We solved this at the introductory meeting by separating "veterans" for the second hour and working up a different, fresh presentation for them. In addition, they were not expected to attend the November small group sessions. Thus, parents who had completed the program in earlier years came only on the first or orientation evening and for the concluding home Mass.

• A ceremony of formal initiation into the program during a Sunday Mass can prove very helpful for both participants and parishioners.

This concept is the adaptation to our own circumstances of an idea encouraged by religious education experts.

As part of the introductory evening we asked the parents to make name tags for their children, signs which not only indicated a boy or girl's name, but also expressed in some visual manner the father's or mother's thoughts about that child. We had our fingers crossed over their reactions, but they responded with enthusiasm to this project and the candidates wore them rather proudly at the following weekend's Eucharist.

At the Sunday celebration parents and children replied after the homily to separate questions inquiring if they were ready to undertake this program of preparation. Then, the boys and girls came with their families to the sanctuary and received from the celebrant a First Communion textbook. "John, receive the good news of Holy Communion."

The huge crowd on hand and the children's excitement indicated we had added something very positive to our program. It also brought out the community's interest in and support of these boys and girls.

• Small group, explanatory home Masses are perhaps the most powerful teaching force in the entire setup.

These begin at 7:00 p.m., continue for one hour and include an explanation of the sacred vessels and vestments, involvement of the youngsters in the liturgy plus a running commentary on the Mass. It is difficult to determine who gains more from this event, the parents or the children.

This year several participants volunteered to bake the special bread used for the occasion and to bring a bottle of suitable wine.

• First Communion with one's family prior to the class celebration can be an especially moving experience.

Many learned and were touched when Sheila Parks and her family, at the little girl's request, received from the cup, when Martha Pfeiffer made First Communion at a Christmas Mass, and when four generations of Flicks joined Kim at the altar for her first reception of the Eucharistic Lord.

Eucharistic Prayers for Children

For many years persons who work extensively with the young pleaded for some changes in the Mass which would make the Eucharist more understandable to little children. They argued that our liturgy has been designed basically for adults and thus those in their early years simply could not comprehend most of what was said or done.

A *Directory for Masses With Children* published by the Vatican in November, 1973, responded to those pleas. It contained very radical principles and numerous practical suggestions for adapting liturgies to the mentality of young people. It also implied that the Holy See would in the near future issue special Eucharistic prayers for children.

Three have now been prepared by Rome and are available for general use throughout the United States.* The introduction to these texts offers some interesting norms to govern their translation and use:

- "The committee of translators should always remember that the Latin text in this case is not intended for liturgical use. Therefore it is not simply to be translated."

"The Latin text determines the purpose, substance, and general form of these prayers, and these should be the same in the translations into various languages. Features proper to the Latin language (which never developed a special style of speaking with children) are never to be carried over into the vernacular texts intended for liturgical use. . . ."

- The celebrant while adapting and following a text adapted to the young should nevertheless avoid a childish style of speaking which could jeopardize the celebration's dignity.

- These texts are designed for Eucharistic celebrations in which the majority of the congregation are children.

- Because of the psychology of children, priests should avoid concelebrating such Masses.

- Certain portions (e.g., the dialogue before the Preface, the Holy, Holy, Holy Lord, and the Consecration formula) are repeated exactly as they occur in the other Eucharistic prayers. This has been done to minimize the differences between adult and children's liturgies as well as to lead young people on to a more mature participation in the Mass.

Eucharistic Prayers for Masses With Children, English translation, copyright © 1975, International Committee on English in the Liturgy, Inc., 1330 Massachusetts Ave., N.W., Washington, DC 20005.

- The structure of these three new texts follows the pattern and normally contains all the elements of a Eucharistic prayer as outlined in the Roman Missal.
- There are more acclamations within each prayer to facilitate participation by the children.

The first Eucharistic prayer for children stresses "simplicity" in style and wording. Consider the phrasing of this memorial after the Consecration:

"We do now what Jesus told us to do. We remember his death and his resurrection and we offer you, Father, the bread that gives us life and the cup that saves us. Jesus brings us to you; welcome us as you welcome him."

The second emphasizes greater "participation." A congregation repeatedly says or sings acclamations like "We praise you, we bless you, we thank you" and "Hosanna in the highest."

The third injects a "variety" into the Eucharistic prayer with variable sections for the different seasons.

For effective use of these new Eucharistic prayers for children, the introduction insists that careful catechetical instruction precede the celebration itself and that priests seek to develop within the young people a reverent, inner, prayerful disposition as they gather for such special Masses.

Eucharistic Prayers for Masses of Reconciliation

I would like here to discuss two new Eucharistic Prayers prepared for Masses of reconciliation* and to answer several frequently raised questions.

Eucharistic Prayers for Masses of Reconciliation, English translation, copyright © 1975, International Committee on English in the Liturgy, Inc.

A Praying and Growing People

Issued in connection with the Holy Year of renewal and reconciliation, those additional Eucharistic Prayers (there are now nine) include their own proper Prefaces.

Phrases in the texts, as we might expect, frequently speak of peace, healing, forgiveness and reconciliation. Consider these excerpts:

"By the power of your Holy Spirit make them one body, healed of all division." (I)

"Your Spirit is at work when understanding puts an end to strife, when hatred is quenched by mercy, and vengeance gives way to forgiveness." (Preface II)

"He is the Word that brings salvation. He is the hand you stretch out to sinners. He is the way that leads to your peace." (II)

"In that new world where the fullness of your peace will be revealed, gather people of every race, language, and way of life to share in the one eternal banquet with Jesus Christ the Lord." (II)

Now to the questions:

"Can we expect additional Vatican-approved Eucharistic Prayers in the future?" Yes.

The 1973 letter on this subject from the Roman Congregation for Divine Worship to national conferences of bishops indicated that the Holy See "will give willing consideration to such requests received from episcopal conferences for new Eucharistic Prayers to be composed for particular needs and introduced into the liturgy" (Paragraph 6).

"How does the Church feel about priests using some of the unauthorized Eucharistic Prayers which are available?" It rather strongly disapproves of the practice.

The same letter states: "Episcopal conferences and individual bishops are strongly asked to lead their priests in a reasonable way to maintain the one practice of the Roman Church" (Paragraph 6).

A later section cites reasons why it opposes use of these unofficial texts and repeats the prohibition:

"Whenever Eucharistic Prayers are used without any approval of the Church's authority, unrest and even dissensions arise, not only among priests, but within the communities themselves, even though the Eucharist should be a 'sign of unity, and the bond of charity.' Many people complain about the overly subjective quality of such texts, and participants have a right to make such a complaint. Otherwise the Eucharistic Prayer, to which they give their assent in the 'Amen' they proclaim, becomes disorderly, or is imbued with the personal feelings of the person who either composes or says it.

"Hence it is necessary to demand that only those Eucharistic Prayers be used which have been approved by the lawful authority of the Church, for they clearly and fully manifest the sentiments of the Church" (Paragraph 11).

"What kind of Eucharistic Prayers do you think are needed today?" I believe we require additional texts to add more variety for our people and ones with more acclamations to bring about greater involvement of the congregation.

Parish leaders who vary the Eucharistic Prayers each Sunday can now offer the congregation a different formula every four, six or even nine weeks. That certainly will help alleviate the routine and repetitious. But further texts, especially if they are nationally composed and deal with the modern scene, could enhance liturgical celebrations.

As a celebrant, my impression is that despite varied Eucharistic Prayers, proper catechesis, good proclamation and appropriate music, congregation members during the canon often look bored, restless or in sort of a dazed daydreaming trance. The insertion of frequent acclamations within the Eucharistic Prayer, as has been done in two of the children's texts, would help overcome these problems which arise when

Private and Public Eucharistic Worship

Would you be troubled, bored, relieved or pleased to learn that a new Vatican decree eliminates, among other things, the both knees, double genuflection before the exposed Blessed Sacrament?

How about a Roman directive which calls for only four to six candles on the altar for exposition of the sacred host in the monstrance instead of the traditional candelabra with their 12 to 14 tapers?

These are relatively minor regulations in a recently issued document, *Holy Communion and Worship of the Eucharist Outside Mass.** It examines, among other topics, the relationship between private prayer to the Blessed Sacrament reserved and public Eucharistic worship.

The ritual says in summary: Private or public prayer before the Blessed Sacrament outside Mass is good in itself and a positive development within the Church. However, "when the faithful honor Christ present in the sacrament, they should remember that this presence is derived from the sacrifice and is directed toward sacramental and spiritual communion" (80).

Those simplified and minor revisions (one knee, not both, four-six candles instead of 12-14) are examples of the reformed rite's practical attempts to preserve a proper perspective in this area. We cite below some others:

- Location of the tabernacle. "A place of some beauty should be chosen for the reservation of the Blessed Sacrament. It should be suitable for private prayer so that the habit of

---

* English translation, copyright © 1974, International Committee on English in the Liturgy, Inc.

paying visits to the Blessed Sacrament may be encouraged. This will be easier if the Blessed Sacrament chapel is separated from the main body of the church, especially where marriages or funerals are a frequent occurrence or where the church is crowded with pilgrims or visitors attracted by its works of art or its antiquity" (9).

- Value of prayer before the tabernacle. "Prayer before Christ the Lord sacramentally present extends the union with Christ which the faithful have reached in Communion. It renews the covenant which in turn moves them to maintain in their lives what they have received by faith and by sacraments. They should try to lead their whole lives with the strength derived from the heavenly food, as they share in the death and resurrection of the Lord" (81).

- Highlighting the Blessed Sacrament. "The presence of the Blessed Sacrament in the tabernacle should be marked by a canopy or some other approved architectural feature" (11). In our day and country, the use of suitable lighting seems one of the more effective methods to achieve this goal.

- Exposition of the Blessed Sacrament is for prayer, not for benediction. "Shorter expositions of the Eucharist are to be arranged in such a way that the blessing with the Eucharist is preceded by a suitable period for readings of the Word of God, songs, prayers and sufficient time for silent prayer.

"Exposition which is held exclusively for the giving of benediction is prohibited" (89).

- Eucharistic devotions should be related to the liturgy. "In the arrangement of devotional services of this kind, the liturgical seasons should be taken into account. Devotions should be in harmony with the sacred liturgy in some sense, take their origin from the liturgy, and lead people back to the liturgy" (79).

A Praying and Growing People 69

- Hosts for the people should be consecrated at the Mass itself, normally not taken from the tabernacle. "The Eucharist is a celebration and to receive Communion during Mass makes the celebration more genuine. At the level of signs this truth can be better appreciated when priest and people share the elements which have just been offered in sacrifice. It should be normal practice at every Eucharist to consecrate bread which has been specially prepared for the people's Communion" (13).

This is not a new directive, but one issued years ago. However, its implementation on the local level throughout the United States leaves much to be desired.

- Dignity of real presence. "His presence as God and man in the sacrament of the Eucharist is without parallel elsewhere: He is wholly and completely present. This is not to deny that Christ is genuinely present in other ways too, but we describe this as the real presence because it is the most personal" (6).

Whatever Happened to Benediction?

Twenty years ago benediction of the Blessed Sacrament held an important part in the devotional life of Roman Catholics. In fact, for many this service seemed to hold greater appeal than Mass itself.

Today, with the multiplication of evening Eucharistic liturgies, a vernacular service in which the congregation can actively participate, and mitigated fast regulations that facilitate reception of Communion, the occasions for benediction have tremendously diminished, even disappeared in some parish churches.

A similar shift in attitude toward the reserved Body and Blood of the Lord can be seen in the Church's official documents over that period which talk about the tabernacle and its proper location within a church.

Jesuit Father Tad Guzie in his book, *Jesus and the Eucharist* (Paulist Press, New York, 1974), summarizes those pronouncements from the Holy See:

"Back in 1957 it was decreed that Mass should be celebrated on the altar where the Eucharist is reserved; a church having only one altar should have the tabernacle on that altar. In 1964 it was decreed that the Eucharist could be reserved on the main altar or on a truly prominent side altar; Masses could be celebrated facing the people even with a tabernacle on the altar. By 1967 the full circle was turned: the tabernacle should not be on the Eucharistic altar; in fact, it should ideally be placed not even in the sanctuary but in a chapel distinct from the central part of the church."

There are persons who deeply regret this demise of devotion to the Blessed Sacrament reserved and the diminution or elimination of occasions for benediction. They see in this trend a weakening of our faith toward the real presence of Christ in the consecrated host.

Others, including some priests, rejoice over the development and a few actually refuse to plan or celebrate benediction in their churches. They consider this devotional practice as detrimental to our belief that Christ is really present in the action of the faith community at Mass.

Pope Paul, in the section already mentioned of the revised Roman Ritual, "Holy Communion and Worship of the Eucharist Outside Mass," steers a typical middle course through this debate.

The document states there is no true conflict between the Mass and benediction or between Holy Communion and the reservation of hosts in a tabernacle. Instead, these can complement one another, if those who plan and execute liturgies observe the proper procedures and keep matters in correct perspective.

I quote the ritual text:

"The celebration of the Eucharist outside Mass springs from and directs Christians back to the Mass itself. During Mass the sacrifice of his life, which is made by Christ the Lord, is one with the life-giving sacrament by which in the form of bread and wine he is present with us. And after Mass in church and oratory he is still 'God with us,' Emmanuel, by the same sacramental presence. Day and night he makes his home with us, full of grace and truth.

"For this reason it may not be doubted that when the faithful honor the Blessed Sacrament, they are offering true worship to the one, true God, as the Catholic Church has always done. The fact that the sacrament was instituted by Christ to be our food should not detract from this truth.

"When the faithful honor Christ present in the sacrament, they should remember that this presence is derived from the sacrifice and is directed toward sacramental and spiritual communion."

QUESTIONS FOR DISCUSSION

1. What do you think is a proper age for a child's First Eucharist? First Penance?
2. How do you feel at Mass as the priest proclaims the Eucharistic Prayer—interested, attentive, bored, restless, distracted, etc? Why?
3. Do you think the tabernacle in your church is located properly? If not, where would you relocate it?

4 A Reconciled People

Sacrament of Reconciliation

One of the last major liturgical revisions following the Second Vatican Council involved the sacrament of Penance. A new rite of reconciliation or "Order of Penance" has now been published, translated into English and made mandatory throughout the United States from the beginning of Lent, 1977.

This restored ritual is specifically designed for the reconciliation of ourselves with God, with one another, and with the world around us.

The reader will find sketched below a few noticeably new features in the liturgy for reconciling individual sinners.

• *Prayer shared by priest and penitent.* Every liturgical book published since Vatican II has arranged worship services in dialogue form. Various persons, in that concept, exercise distinct roles—e.g., celebrant, lector, server, congregation. The priest is not the only one who speaks; it is expected that those present participate, at least by a verbal response.

The reformed rite for Penance follows a similar pattern.

At the beginning, the priest is directed to greet the penitent in a kind manner and with understanding words. The ritual suggests that both make the sign of the cross and that the celebrant pray for the sinner spontaneously or with one of several supplied formulas.

After the confession and absolution, there is likewise a brief, prayerful dialogue, a proclamation praising God whose limitless mercy will last forever.

In addition, the flexible rite offers throughout the celebration opportunities for confessor and penitent to pray together in a quite personal way about the sinner's situation.

• *Reading from sacred scripture.* Before the confession of sins and the acceptance of a penance, the priest either recites from memory or reads from a printed text with the penitent some section of the bible. This passage announces God's great mercy and summons the sinner to a conversion or change of heart.

That remains an optional step, but one highly desirable and certainly envisioned by the Church, which lists in its ritual over 100 scriptural excerpts suitable for the purpose.

• *An act of contrition.* In recent years, penitents have often been encouraged to make the traditional act of contrition either before or after confession itself. With a vernacular absolution it seemed best for the sinner to listen and hear that pronouncement of forgiveness.

The revised rite, however, now invites the penitent to verbalize this inner repentance in his or her own words or according to one of the 10 formulas provided.

The confessor delays proclaiming the words of absolution until that act of contrition has been completed.

• A new absolution formula. This simpler form brings out more explicitly the action of the Holy Spirit in the sacrament and the Church's part in this reconciliation process.

• Imposition of hands. While speaking the phrases of forgiveness, a confessor imposes his hands upon the head of the penitent or at least extends his right hand toward the sinner.

The restoration of that ancient gesture recalls, of course, the way in which a bishop during those first centuries reconciled individual sinners who had removed themselves from the Christian community. So too today, the confessor, representing the chief shepherd of a diocese, welcomes back a sinner cut off from or but weakly attached to the Body of Christ and the People of God.

Finding Sins to Confess

"Bless me Father, it has been a long time since I went to confession—maybe nine months or even a year. I feel guilty about putting it off this way, but I haven't done anything very bad and don't know what to say or tell."

That sin-free, yet still troubled penitent speaks for many Roman Catholics in the United States today. These are relatively good Christians, persons leading admirable lives, but disturbed deep down that they have neglected what once was a regular, frequent part of their religious routine.

The reformed procedure for the new rite of Penance, rich and flexible as it is, will touch only indirectly the problem our person mentioned above. That difficulty—how to make "devotional confessions" come alive—can be solved, I believe, only by joint efforts of confessors and penitents. They need to develop together a fresh, scripture-oriented approach toward the examination of conscience and expression of sin.

This development, simply stated, seeks to uncover one or two dominant inner sinful attitudes or evil dispositions of the heart. It does not try to compile a list of venial sins with exact numbers attached to each category.

Moreover, it challenges the penitent to compare his or her life with the ideals sketched by Jesus in the gospel. Such a confrontation moves beyond, without excluding, the kinds of sins we usually have mentioned in the past.

The latter confession may include, for example, lies, uncharitable remarks, impatient behavior, improper thoughts. The former, to illustrate, would cite a general unwillingness to forgive one who has hurt us, constant neglect of some relative confined to the local nursing home, an excessive concern about making money.

Preparation for these types of confessions obviously demands time and reflection, items often unavailable or unattractive in this busy, noisy contemporary society of ours.

Penitents will also require assistance from confessors or teachers, particularly in the beginning, and may find some type of booklet or manual equally necessary.

A publication, *Together in Peace,* written by this author (Ave Maria Press, Notre Dame, Indiana 46556), seeks to provide penitents with such a biblically based, disposition-oriented "Look into the Heart."

It suggests, in that section, 12 areas of concern (e.g., "Service or Neglect of Others," "The Law of Love," "Correcting Another," "A Call to Prayer"). Within each area, the text offers several pertinent passages from sacred scripture plus a few remarks designed to stimulate a reflective look at the past.

The penitent would select on a given occasion only one or two of these topics, read the appropriate material, compare those ideals with his or her past weeks or months and then mentally prepare a confession of sinfulness.

That account would tend, consequently, to take a more general, attitudinal form, a revealing of the dispositions and causes behind sins rather than the sins themselves. Sins, here, are seen more as symptoms of an evil within us which calls for God's and the Church's cleansing and healing.

Sensitivity to Sin

Human nature does not seem to change much over the centuries. The temptations, weaknesses and failures we read about in the Old Testament days of Saul and David are not radically different from those of the 1970's.

Saul became jealous of David. He grew very angry and resentful when crowds praised the young leader by singing, "Saul has slain his thousands, and David his ten thousands." The King likewise raged in his house over the youth's popularity and eventually sought to kill him.

David, later, also knew weakness and sin. He took another man's wife and then, as is often the case, compounded this fall by arranging for the wronged husband's death.

Critics warned both Saul and David, pricked their consciences, told them they were wrong.

Jonathan pleaded with his father, Saul: "Let not your majesty sin against his servant David."

The prophet Nathan told David: "You are the man! . . . Why have you spurned the Lord and done evil in his sight?"

Some observers of the contemporary scene, like psychiatrist Karl Menninger, believe we need a few more Jonathans and Nathans today. They feel that modern men and women, for various reasons, have grown insensitive to sin and either are not aware of their moral faults or too easily rationalize them away.

An appendix in the new Rite for Penance contains an examination of conscience which might help in this regard.

In a positive, but pointed, way it examines three divine commands: "You shall love the Lord your God with your whole heart," "Love one another as I have loved you," and "Be perfect as your Father is perfect." Under each mandate, the examination poses a lengthy series of questions designed to stimulate our consciences and increase our awareness of sin.

I think Roman Catholics might find daily use of this section an excellent moral sensitizer in their individual lives. The appendix includes 24 paragraphs of questions. Taking one each night could, over several months, lead the concerned

A Reconciled People

individual to a much keener view of what it means to be a Christian.

Here are samplings of that text:

Under number I, "You shall love the Lord your God with your whole heart":

"Is my heart set on God, so that I really love him above all things and am faithful to his commandments, as a son loves his father? Or am I more concerned about the things of this world? Have I a right intention in what I do?"

Under number II, "Love one another as I have loved you":

"Am I concerned for the good and prosperity of the human community in which I live, or do I spend my life caring only for myself? Do I share to the best of my ability in the work of promoting justice, morality, harmony, and love in human relations? Have I done my duty as a citizen? Have I paid my taxes?"

Under number III, "Be perfect as your Father is perfect":

"Where is my life really leading me? Is the hope of eternal life my inspiration? Have I tried to grow in the life of the Spirit through prayer, reading the Word of God and meditating on it, receiving the sacraments, self-denial? Have I been anxious to control my vices, my bad inclinations and passions, e.g., envy, love of food and drink? Have I been proud and boastful, thinking myself better in the sight of God and despising others as less important than myself? Have I imposed my own will on others, without respecting their freedom and rights?"

Remodeled Confessionals

A directive in the Introduction of the revised ritual for Penance reveals an interesting development. It states:

"Following this prayer, the priest extends his hands, or at least his right hand, over the head of the penitent and pronounces the formula of absolution. . . ."

How the confessor can extend either both or at least his right hand over the penitent's head in our customary "boxes" is a good question. Later the actual rubric does slightly modify this point, indicating as an alternative that he "at least extends his right hand." That procedure clearly is possible in the standard confessional.

In a similarly flexible manner, introductory directions suggest: "Then the priest, or the penitent himself, may read a text of holy scripture, or this may be done as part of the preparation for the sacrament."

Again, it would be nearly impossible for me to have done this last Saturday in our "box"; however, I easily did it in our room of reconciliation.

The reformed ritual does not speak in any detail about the kind of space which will be the normal location for the celebration of Penance. It merely notes that "the sacrament of Penance is celebrated in the place and location prescribed by law" (number 12).

However, a later article, number 38, indicates, "it is the responsibility of episcopal conferences in this matter . . . to determine more precise regulations about the place proper for the ordinary celebration of the sacrament of Penance . . . ."

The National Conference of Catholic Bishops for the United States, responding to that directive of the ritual, approved at its November, 1974, meeting the following resolution:

> . . . That it be considered desirable that small chapels or rooms of reconciliation be provided in which penitents might choose to confess their sins and seek sacramental reconciliation through an informal face-to-face exchange with the priest, with the opportunity for appropriate

spiritual counsel. It would also be regarded as desirable that such chapels or rooms be designed to afford the option of the penitent's kneeling at the fixed confessional grill in the usual way, but in every case the freedom of the penitent is to be respected.

In a letter dated October 11, 1975, James Cardinal Knox, Prefect of the Sacred Congregation for the Sacraments and Divine Worship, writing to our Archbishop Joseph Bernardin, president of the NCCB, supported that resolution.

I am happy to reply to your letter regarding norms determining the place for the ordinary celebration of the sacrament of Penance. This Congregation has carefully studied the provisions approved by the National Conference of Catholic Bishops in this regard, and is happy to confirm what the Bishops approved.

What can be done with existing churches to provide at reasonable cost such reconciliation spaces? There are several immediate possibilities:

- Some readers will recall our room of reconciliation at Holy Family as described in my columns and pictured in the priest's edition of *Together in Peace*. We converted a relatively unused room off one entrance into such an attractive, softly lighted area. Here penitents can confess either kneeling or sitting behind a wooden grate or sitting face to face across a table from the priest.

- A former baptistery (with the font moved to the sanctuary) in many instances can be transformed without great difficulty into a permanent reconciliation area.

- Crying rooms (already soundproofed, obviously) and sacristies become, with suitable drapes and movable furniture, satisfactory temporary locations for the celebration of Penance.

- A traditional two-penitent confessional can be changed into a small, slightly crowded room of reconciliation for one penitent in which the various necessary options are provided for each person.

I have before me two blueprints with designs by Robert Rambusch of a "Remodeled Confession for Reconciliation Rites." The New York artist takes the traditional two-penitent confessional, knocks out old partitions and adds a few new ones, then suggests draw curtain, wall lamp, priest's swivel and penitent's straight chair, plus a prie-dieu. These simple renovations thus present parishioners with a quite inexpensive reconciliation space.

Where there is sufficient passageway area, Rambusch slightly enlarges the arrangement by pushing the reconciliation walls out 16 inches into the aisle. In both circumstances the draw curtain is controlled by the penitent who can confess behind it with perfect anonymity or pull the drape aside and converse in a face-to-face manner with the priest.

The essential element in any room of reconciliation is this freedom or option offered penitents to select that method —anonymous or face-to-face, kneeling or sitting—which they find most comfortable and conducive to a personal meeting with Christ their Savior.

Full and effective use of the new liturgy and these areas for Penance will require more time than it did in the past. We will discuss that challenge next.

Longer, but Better Confessions

Waiting in line to confess your sins is not one of life's more enjoyable experiences. With the general decline in the number and frequency of persons approaching the sacrament of Penance, that phenomenon occurs much less often than it did a decade or two ago. Nevertheless, the uncomfortable standing and shifting from one foot to the other, the generally anxious feeling about what must be said and will happen remains.

Those sentiments hardly serve as the best preparation for a peace-filled meeting with Christ in this sacramental encounter.

Certain aspects of the reversed ritual for Penance suggest that our confessions in the future may take a bit longer than heretofore, at least if celebrated according to the full and ideal arrangement.

Praying with the priest, sharing a biblical reading or two, getting to the root cause of our sinfulness, reciting an act of contrition, agreeing upon a suitable, creative, constructive task of satisfaction—all these take a few moments of time. When combined they total more than the past, brief, in-and-out, 60-second procedures.

Moreover, the optional face-to-face type of confessions possible in the reconciliation areas previously described tend to require a slightly longer period of time. In the five years we have used our room at Holy Family, 85 percent of those selecting this space over the "box" opted for an across-the-table, open process. Penitents following this method do, in fact, normally move beyond a simple listing of sins and seek to reveal the "why" behind their failures.

That, of course, can prove healing and helpful for the penitent with the priest, but a bit nerve-racking, even exasperating for those who wait outside.

Is there any way to ease such a difficulty?

We have found no easy solution, surely no perfect answer. Here are however, some possibilities:

• Chairs, an FM radio playing soft, suitable background music, a table with available literature (e.g., paperback bible, *Together in Peace*) can turn a negative, time-wasting period into a positive, disposition-building session.

One penitent, forced during a particularly crowded pre-feast confessional time to wait for nearly an hour, found the music eased his nervousness and a pamphlet gave him added inspiration.

• More flexible and convenient scheduled hours may reduce the pressure on those traditional Saturday afternoon and evening periods. Mornings, the day before Ash Wednesday and Thanksgiving, at wakes or by appointment are some of the rather unusual occasions we have found popular.

• Priest and penitent need to understand the difference between the sacrament of Penance and a counseling session. The distinction admittedly is harder to determine in cases during which a penitent seeks to reveal his or her basic disposition and to discover the root causes behind the sins confessed.

Still, a wise confessor and a considerate penitent (especially if aware of persons waiting their turn outside) could postpone to another occasion a more detailed discussion of certain matters.

• If most parishioners developed a habit of celebrating this sacrament every three months or four times a year (like the former Ember days) according to the revised ritual, priests would probably be busy, but not overwhelmed.

• Priests may need to reorient their priorities. Few pastoral efforts bear such abundant spiritual fruit and it would not be a bad development for the Church if we found the demand brought us back to this task which consumed so many hours in the recent past.

Roman Catholics today deserve the opportunity to make rich receptions of Penance a frequent part of their lives.

Fears and Tears

We celebrate the sacrament of Penance at Holy Family, among other times, between 4:00 and 5:00 p.m. on Saturdays, concluding just prior to that afternoon's anticipated Sunday Mass.

A few weeks ago I finished this hour of hearing confessions in our reconciliation room, waited a moment for any latecomers, turned off two floor lamps and walked out into the vestibule-waiting area.

There I saw a little girl clinging to her mother, hiding behind dad and sobbing her heart out.

The father nervously smiled and said: "Mary wants to make her second confession, Father, but she has forgotten the act of contrition and is afraid to go."

If Mary's fears and tears developed because she didn't know the priest or had received a harsh, rigid training in preparation for this sacrament, her fears would be understandable.

However, the little girl in other circumstances would not hesitate to give me a child's hug and kiss; she sees, waves, smiles each Sunday at Mass; Mary was there when I censused the home and visited with her parents; she probably even made her first confession to me.

Moreover, our formation program is positive, low key, through the parents and with emphasis on God's loving kindness, not on strict memorization of formulas or procedures.

Still tears and fears.

After the experience of a nearly yearlong preparation for our parishioners on the revised rite of Penance, I am beginning to wonder if many adult Catholics may not react in a somewhat similar, although obviously less intense, fashion to the new ritual.

The procedure is neither complicated nor tightly regulated. There are, true enough, multiple choices and various options, but, at the same time, great freedom to be oneself and heavy emphasis on the spirit of reconciliation, rather than on the external rite.

Nevertheless, I am concerned some will just throw up their hands in disgust or confusion at the change and find they now have an additional reason to avoid this great sacrament of peace.

That problem merely underscores the need for a patient, repeated, lengthy instruction of parishioners on the what, how and why of this restored ceremony.

Sunday Masses and the weekly bulletin still represent the best vehicles for such a catechesis. Study groups, first Penance parental preparation courses, lecture series, etc., on the subject all have their value and each parish needs them. But the great mass of people will be reached by the weekend Eucharist, not by these other instructional methods.

A series of homilies—six seems a minimum—delivered with a month's interval between each one should cover topics like sin (with reference to the fall in Genesis), conversion or reconciliation, the use of sacred scripture in the new rite, sacramental signs in the revised ritual, Penance as a means of spiritual growth, and communal penance services.

A paragraph in the bulletin which either prepares people for next week's explanatory sermon or expands on a topic treated in a previous homily enhances the effectiveness of those spoken words.

Finally, a few handouts, distributed after Mass, which contain an outline of the Rite for Reconciliation of individual penitents and a description of communal penance liturgies could deepen parishioners' understanding of matters explained in a necessarily limited way by the 10-minute homily and abbreviated bulletin commentaries.

At the request of several priests throughout the country,

this writer prepared a text, *Preparing for the New Rite of Penance: A Homily and Teaching Guide* (Ave Maria Press, Notre Dame, Indiana 46556, $1.50) which includes those items. The booklet contains six homilies with detailed outlines, 30 instructional bulletin paragraphs and three copy-ready handouts. It also offers a few guiding principles for this catechesis of our people.

Communal Penance Services

"No man is an island," the saying goes, but, in a sense, every man is an island.

Each individual influences other persons and is influenced by them. At the same time, we always remain unique, independent human beings never totally absorbed by the group or fully understood by others.

That fundamental tension between the individual and the community manifests itself in the new communal rite for the sacrament of Penance.

The ceremony is entitled "Rite for Reconciliation of Several Penitents with Individual Confession and Absolution."

A section from the introduction to the ritual summarizes the purpose of such a service:

"Communal celebration shows more clearly the ecclesial nature of Penance. The faithful listen together to the Word of God, which proclaims his mercy and invites them to conversion; at the same time they examine the conformity of their lives with that Word of God and help each other through common prayer. After each person has confessed his sins and received absolution, all praise God together for his wonderful deeds on behalf of the people he has gained for himself through the blood of his Son."

The tension we noted develops during the period when

each person confesses his or her sins. That is, of course, a highly individualistic action and the amount of time required will vary greatly from person to person. Even with a plentiful supply of priests available, the relation of sins and discussion with a confessor may extend for a lengthy interval.

For those who have already confessed and await the ceremony's conclusion, that delay can produce boredom and restlessness. For those still waiting to confess, the delay creates an uncomfortable pressure which destroys some of the celebration's effectiveness and may prompt them to rush or even skip the confession.

The priests likewise experience a tension in this arrangement. Trained to view the sacrament of Penance as a delicate, personal event and to view each penitent as a singular individual, they may find the need to speed along and offer little advice. This is extremely frustrating.

Similarly, when instructed beforehand by the planners to ask no questions and give no guidance, simply to recite the words of absolution, some confessors see themselves reduced to mechanical absolving machines.

We have tried to ease (one does not resolve) this conflict between the individual and the communal by preparing two types of Penance services.

The first includes all the typical elements—common song, prayer, readings, etc.—but never really concludes. After the sign of peace and Our Father, we invite participants either to sit in church and reflect on the peace experienced through the service, or to step downstairs for coffee, cookies, conversation and a continuation of the reconciliation achieved by the ceremony, or to meet Christ in the sacrament of Penance by confessing to one of the many priests available.

These liturgies have not attracted huge crowds—perhaps 50 to 150—but the confessions afterwards were of high quality and lasted for perhaps an hour. Neither priest nor penitent

A Reconciled People

felt rushed and if the lines were long or the delay lengthy, one could walk downstairs for refreshments and return later.

The weakness of this plan is the absence of a communal song and prayer at the end celebrating the congregation's joy and reconciliation.

Our second communal Penance service follows the new rite exactly and at the specified moment those who wish choose their confessor from among the many priests present.

Advance publicity promises and the priests observe a procedure in which few, if any, questions are asked and little or no counsel given.

During the "confession portion," those in the congregation sing appropriate hymns, recite suitable prayers (like the Reproaches of Good Friday) and listen to choral or instrumental music. We encourage them to utilize this "waiting period" as an occasion of prayer for their brothers and sisters about to meet Jesus in the sacrament of Penance.

A Palm Sunday afternoon celebration of this second type attracted a community of 400 individuals who helped one another and rejoiced with one another over Christ's forgiveness and peace.

Expectations of a Confessor

What do you expect of the priest who hears your confession?

Do you, as a woman, hope he will hold you in the delicate regard Jesus did during a period of history when women were not treated so delicately?

Do you anticipate the priest will be a leader, friend and patient teacher in much the same way that Christ was leader, friend and patient teacher to the Apostles?

Borrowing a technique from two Chicago colleagues, I

asked a group of priests from Kansas City, Kansas, plus mixed audiences in Salinas and Atascadero, California, to write down anonymously their expectations of a confessor. The extremely honest, reflective responses indirectly give us a good contemporary picture of the ideal priest who celebrates the sacrament of Penance.

- Availability and interest were at the top of the list. "As a priest I just want him to be available for confession—all too often we get the feeling today we are only tolerated by our brother priests especially when our confessions are primarily devotional."

"Is he glad I came? Does he show it? Is he interested in me as a person, in how I feel and hurt? Does he listen?"

- Allowing the penitent ample time was another frequent answer.

A parent wrote: "Someone who doesn't rush me. After getting up my courage to go to confession, I need time." A Kansas City priest looks for "a priest who listens, who never butts in when I am talking." Another from that diocese expects in the priest "a sense that it is important to be celebrating the sacrament of Penance and that I am not interrupting his 'busy' schedule."

- Almost every respondent manifested a need for encouragement.

A lay person at Salinas remarked: "Once a priest said Jesus must love you very much. I think of that so very often when I feel tempted."

This observation came from a priest religious: "At my age (69) I want a confessor who would encourage me and give me a more vivid sense of faith. He should put me in a more personal touch with Christ, but, perhaps, what is more important, give me greater assurance that I am in God's good graces."

- Some mentioned their desire for a patient, nonscolding approach.

"As a priest I need a confessor who is kindly, tolerant of my sometimes clumsy way of expressing things."

A sister pleaded: "Confession has not been easy for me. I have already scolded myself and I don't need another. I want to be told in words that God loves me."

- The following expectation which occurred a few times interested me: "I look for one who is conscious of his own sins and gives the appearance of weakness, not one who appears strong."

- An updated, firm, prayerful, wise confessor.

A sister in California wrote of her hope for one "who realizes life is not stagnant, but full of tensions, who keeps himself updated, who is as deeply spiritual and prayerful a person as possible."

A priest from the same area observed: "St. Teresa of Avila, when asked whether she would choose a holy or a smart confessor, said, 'a smart one.' So would I. He also should be firm, but never forget sins are an offense against God and not against him."

Two final comments of interest from lay persons:

"A friendly welcome, nonjudgmental listening, nonmechanical praying, a feeling that I'm a unique person. He must be present, not going through the motions. Must it be a priest?"

"I am not sure I expect anything from the confessor. At the present time I do not use the sacrament of Penance because as a young person it stirred up so much guilt in me as to not be helpful but rather a hindrance to emotional balance. I am very much interested in the face-to-face concept you describe. Then I would expect attentive, receptive listening."

Three Common Questions About Reconciliation

Three questions about the new rite of Penance keep coming to the surface as I speak on this topic around the country:

Is private confession going to disappear?

Will all our confessional boxes be removed?

Can we expect general or group absolution without individual confession to become the common or ordinary practice for the United States?

I think we can safely respond "no" to all three inquiries.

Disappearance of Private Confession

Far from disappearing, I look for a resurgence of interest in individual, auricular confession with an accompanying rise in the number of persons finding this sacramental experience a source of spiritual healing and growth.

Certainly that is the mind of the Church and the intention of the revised ritual.

Paragraph 7 of the text's introduction reads:

"Moreover, frequent and careful celebration of this sacrament is also very useful as a remedy for venial sins. This is not a mere ritual repetition or psychological exercise, but a serious striving to perfect the grace of Baptism so that, as we bear in our body the death of Jesus Christ, his life may be seen in us ever more clearly. In confession of this kind, penitents who accuse themselves of venial faults should try to conform more closely to Christ and to follow the voice of the Spirit more attentively.

"In order that this sacrament of healing may truly achieve its purpose among Christ's faithful, it must take root in their whole lives and move them to more fervent service of God and neighbor."

In addition, the actual Rite for Reconciliation of individual penitents contains various possibilities, including a variety of prayers and scriptural readings, designed to make so-called "private" confessions richer and more effective.

Removal of Familiar Confessional "Boxes"

These traditional spaces for individual confession of sins will probably give way in time to reconciliation rooms. However, in the immediate future for most churches and for years to come in some parishes, the one or two penitent areas normally built into the side or near walls will certainly remain. But even in those forward-moving congregations which swiftly develop handsome rooms for this sacrament, penitents should have the option of anonymity.

The National Conference of Catholic Bishops in the United States through a recent decision quoted in an earlier section both encouraged the construction of reconciliation chapels while insisting that the freedom of a person to confess anonymously be preserved.

General Absolution

The new ritual includes a liturgy for general absolution without individual confession of sins and sets guidelines when this procedure is to be allowed.

Nevertheless, it states: "Individual, integral confession and absolution remain the only ordinary way for the faithful to reconcile themselves with God and the Church, unless physical or moral impossibility excuses from this kind of confession" (Art. 31).

Moreover, even when the local bishop approves of this for a specific situation, those "who receive pardon for grave sins by a common absolution should go to individual confession before they receive this kind of absolution again, unless they are impeded by a just reason" (Art. 34).

While general absolution without individual confession may become a more common way of reconciling persons with persons and persons with God than it has in the past century, the Church does not envision this as the ordinary procedure or one which will replace individual telling of sins to the priest.

QUESTIONS FOR DISCUSSION

1. Why do people tend to stay away from confession or the sacrament of Penance?
2. Describe the kind of person you want the priest to be when you confess your sins.

5 A Loving People

Symbol of the Wedding Ring

"Mary, take this ring as a sign of my love and fidelity. In the name of the Father, and of the Son, and of the Holy Spirit."

Since most couples in my experience over the past 10 years have opted for a double-ring ceremony, Mary, after accepting this gift and drawing it farther onto the third finger left hand, will probably reciprocate and give a similar wedding band to her spouse.

The rings signify, of course, that Mary and her partner are now husband and wife, married, joined legally and spiritually.

But those nuptial bands normally bear a deeper meaning and communicate, especially to the wearers, much more than the mere external fact of marriage.

They should and usually do symbolize all kinds of inner qualities, attitudes and feelings.

The rings say in effect: "I love you, I am committed to you, I will care about you throughout the future in both good and bad times, in sickness and health, in joys and sorrows."

They also can spark in one individual swift and spontaneous thoughts about the other; stir memories of shared tears and common laughter; recall moments the partners hurt each other and times they made love.

These rings may likewise serve as a source of courage and strength when temptation or adversity places the original commitment under strain.

For example. A husband away at length from home, weary after tension-filled days, discouraged by business frustrations, lonely and vulnerable, is tempted by an obvious invitation. He feels weak and finds the offer very attractive, but a glance at or touch of his ring changes the picture and carries him through that temporary crisis.

Another illustration: an exhausted wife struggles to cope with her cancer-ridden, dying husband. His constant, changing, imperative day-and-night requests test the woman's endurance. She, too, fingers her wedding band and in a silent, mysterious way finds there power to continue.

The nuptial rings as signs (I am married) do not deeply touch our inner selves; however, as symbols (I love, care, am committed) they can evoke a variety of strong conscious and unconscious reactions within us.

Father Avery Dulles in his *Models of the Church* explains this strange power of symbols in psychological terms and applies that explanation to specifically religious images.

He maintains these symbols find an echo in the inarticulate depths of a person's psyche. They communicate through their evocative power and convey a latent meaning. Such symbols transform the horizons of an individual's life, alter one's scale of values, reorient loyalties. We apprehend them not simply by the mind but by the imagination, the heart, or better, by the whole man.

In Dulles' words, "they suggest attitudes and courses of action; they intensify confidence and devotion."

We sometimes speak of the Incarnation in the language of marriage, wondering over the love which prompted God to wed our humanity.

The nuptial rings communicate much more to us than the

cold fact that a marriage has taken place. They stir feelings and attitudes within our total being, provoke conscious and unconscious reactions, drive home the great implications of that wedding which began at Nazareth and continued in Bethlehem.

Marriage Encounter

About 20 of our couples in the parish have recently completed a marriage encounter. For readers who may have never heard of the movement or who are turned off by the "hugging and kissing" of encountered couples or who feel interested, but apprehensive, about the 44-hour weekend event, here are some observations.

From what I understand, the encounter is to make good marriages better, not to save sour unions or work miracles for emotionally troubled persons; couples will not understand what the weekend is unless they experience it themselves; participants return almost universally positive and highly enthusiastic about their encounter; couples manifest a sudden and profound growth in love for others, interest in the parish, joy in their hearts.

The latter points, particularly this new concern for others and willingness to serve, speak rather convincingly to me. Joy and a swift urge of emotional enthusiasm are, of course, good signs, but often they fade fast and lack staying power. Unselfish love, on the other hand, is a sure sign of God's presence in a person or movement.

In the past few years I have witnessed several remarkable incidents of that self-giving spirit among encountered couples

• I met after 17 years the first couple whose marriage ceremony I had performed as a young priest. They were and are delightful persons, but the husband was never a particularly faithful Catholic nor the wife much of a practicing Protestant. Marriage encounter changed that and they drove 40 miles with their family on a Sunday afternoon to tell me this.

• On a trip to Philadelphia's Malvern Retreat House for a next-day lecture, I stopped at a restaurant for a quick dinner alone. Several happy couples and a priest spotted the unknown cleric sitting by himself and invited me over for dinner.

They had just concluded "giving" an encounter and, again, I heard testimony of persons alienated from the Church now reconciled and active in it. Afterwards (following the usual warm embraces) one couple, despite inconvenience, drove me to the retreat house and later wrote me a beautiful letter about our meeting.

• At an information night in our parish, an out-of-town husband spoke quietly to me of how he made his first confession in eight years during a weekend encounter.

• One of our couples with 10 children was anxious to make an encounter, but understandingly concerned about care of the boys and girls for those Friday-Sunday hours.

No problem. An encountered couple from a nearby city with five of their own took the 10 and, aided by others, hosted them for the entire weekend.

Love begets love. Upon their return our newly encountered, visibly changed and highly enthusiastic parents of 10, a few weekends later, hosted another family of youngsters while their dad and mom made the weekend.

• "Tom, have you noticed any difference in your parents since they made the weekend encounter?" My fifth-grade altar boy smiled, nodded yes, and replied they were much friendlier.

• Archbishop Whealon of Hartford, following his own encounter weekend, wrote: "Marriage encounter is a powerful spiritual and human experience, deserving highest recommendation to couples of all ages, to priests and religious. It is also a force—I hope and pray—to be reckoned with in parish life of the future."

Solomon asked God only for an understanding heart. He received that from the Lord and much more besides.

Couples approaching a marriage encounter who make a similar request apparently likewise receive that and much more besides.

One-to-One Pre-Cana

One of my bigger surprises and disappointments in the priestly ministry has been pre-Cana or marriage preparation sessions. I looked forward a few years after ordination with great anticipation to my first experience before a group of engaged couples. After all, they were young, in love, and presumably anxious to hear words of wisdom about the sacrament of Matrimony; I, too, was young, supposedly related fairly well to people of that age bracket and enjoyed speaking on this topic. Then came the shock. Most of the 50-plus couples sat sullen and silent, arms folded, eyes on the clock, feet shuffling back and forth under the chairs. Jokes which normally drew strong laughter hardly brought a smile. Questions were few and far between. There was no applause, no thank-yous, no warm fuzzies at the end, only a rapid departure from the auditorium.

That painful opening encounter has repeated itself at many pre-Cana meetings since then. Anonymous feedback forms indicated that despite the hostile and nonresponsive atmosphere and reception, the couples in fact liked our presentations and benefited from them. But it certainly was difficult to judge this from the initial reaction or external appearances. Aware of such an apparent reluctance, even resentment upon the part of engaged persons, we invited with some hesitation married couples at Holy Family to join in a special one-to-one marriage preparation program. The results, however, have been extremely positive.

We present a young man and woman several options when they come to the rectory and set a definite date for their wedding: travel to Syracuse or Oswego for a diocesan pre-Cana conference; participate in an Engaged Encounter weekend; meet with one of our own couples for a few hours. Most select the latter. After the engaged make this choice, the married couple assigned contacts them and invites the young lovers to their home at a mutually acceptable time. The format for that afternoon or evening is quite unstructured. During the several hours they visit, the married couple attempts to guide the easy, free-flowing discussion over about 10 topics which include love, communication, finances, inlaws, sex, children, forgiveness and religion.

It is hard to say who is more nervous at the beginning—the engaged or the married couple. Nevertheless, the tension quickly seems to dissolve, common bonds are swiftly discovered and the conversation proceeds from one subject to the next without much difficulty. Our 10 pre-Cana couples happen to be marriage encounter persons. They were the only ones who volunteered, although the opportunity was and is open to any married individual in the parish. Their encounter weekend and later experiences seemed to help these couples with our one-to-one program. Having discussed at length with each other and with similar people in the movement these basic issues of marriage, they felt more comfortable in articulating those questions to the engaged couple.

In addition, they allowed the young lovers to talk and avoided lecturing to them. Moreover, they conveyed genuine interest and joy in the couple, indicating how much they benefited from the engaged persons' sharing of their inner selves with them. Married couples like this are able to make points about the Church and religion more effectively than we as priests can do. Those who seldom participate in Sunday Mass expect the clergy to say something about that—it is our "job"; similar words from concerned lay people have greater impact.

Larry Morrell and Barbara Pisano were all smiles after a one-to-one marriage preparation "visit" with the Foleys. They smiled all over again when, in response to their invitation, that couple came to the wedding and the reception which followed.

A Policy for Early Marriages

"Father, I would like to make an appointment with you. Sam and I are having a little trouble in our marriage." The caller is a pleasant woman in her early 20s, married to equally likeable Sam in a church ceremony two or three years earlier.

Priests (I presume ministers and rabbis as well) across the country have been swamped with similar telephone messages in the past decade. It is not a new experience—troubled couples often turned to their parish clergy for guidance and support long before the current marital crisis developed; but the increasing frequency of those pleas for help is a new and disturbing phenomenon. Those calls, however, merely reflect national statistics which indicate an apparently vast amount of unhappiness in many marriages. This is particularly true of nuptial unions involving the very young.

The Family Life Division of our bishops' United States Catholic Conference reports that 50 percent of marriages involving teenagers end in failure and for those in which a pregnancy is part of the picture, the disaster rate zooms to 90 percent. For starry-eyed young lovers or anxious parents of a pregnant teenage girl, those statistics do not carry much force. They respond: our case is different; we are the exceptions; their love will last; marriage holds the only answer. The prophets Elijah and Elisha, like prophets before and after, found it difficult to swim against the current, to stem the tide of paganism engulfing God's people in their day. Those who seek with good reason to delay a couple unwisely intent on marriage suffer a similar fate in today's world.

Nevertheless, the Church must, at times, speak forcefully and take strong steps even if those words and actions go contrary to the prevailing climate or culture. Our diocese, like many others in the nation, has recently established some quite specific directives in an effort to reduce the number of marital disasters, especially among the very young. All couples, for example, must contact the parish priest at least three months prior to the wedding date. This will provide ample time for interviews, discussion and premarriage instructions.

I, for one, certainly welcome such diocesan level norm. It takes the local clergy off the hook, so to speak, when an engaged couple show up at the door and wish to be married within a week or two. Since all the other detailed arrangements have been completed, this prospective bride and groom obviously left until last the Church's and their spiritual preparation. Publication of this regulation should in time make those contemplating marriage aware that the Catholic Church considers matrimony a serious step requiring a certain amount of preliminary religious effort on the engaged couple's part.

The diocesan directives also bluntly state: Couples are not allowed "to marry if one or the other or both are under 18." It presumes such a young man and woman are not mature enough for marriage. Nevertheless, they do have recourse and if, after a complicated, but no longer than four-month counseling process, they can convince the bishop of their maturity and readiness, they will be granted permission for the ceremony.

The purpose of these directives is not, obviously, to make eager young couples miserable (although they probably will feel that way in the beginning), but to spare them later, permanent, more serious marital misery. In the words of our bishop: "The essence of this policy is to express the concern of the Church for young people and to assure them the opportunity to prove to themselves that they are able to enter a marriage, the strength and permanence of which will reflect to their own good and the good of all the people of God."

There will still be calls from persons like Sam or his wife after this policy has been in operation, but perhaps they will not be as numerous or as frequent.

The One-Parent Family Council

"Father, we are just a group of lonely people who get together for support." Those words came from the lips of a woman in her 40s, divorced, mother of several and member of the One-Parent Family Council in a neighboring city. I spoke about divorce and remarriage to some 40 to 50 persons of that group gathered on a Thursday night for their monthly meeting held in the dining room of a local hotel.

In operation since 1974, the One-Parent Family Council seeks to provide "a gathering point for area parents who, because of death, divorce, separation or desertion, are forced to depend solely on their own resources to maintain a good life for themselves and their children. The Council hopes to aid in this endeavor by (1) helping the parent to adjust successfully to his or her new situation, and (2) exploring the needs of child and parent in the one-parent household."

This is not a Catholic group, although many present were in practice or allegiance Roman Catholic. But the organization, or one similar to it, certainly deserves the

Church's strong encouragement. The monthly meetings include a brief business session, a speaker or special program, followed by an After-Glow of dancing/socializing. Between those regular gatherings, the officers attempt to plan one social activity each weekend.

Sundays seem to present one of the most painful periods for the woman in a one-parent situation. The ex-husband and father normally enjoys visitation rights on that day, leaving her at home — alone and lonely. Going to movies, concerts, plays, lectures and other events for entertainment is another difficult time. Instead of renewing the one-parent's spirits, those occasions often depress them. "Do you realize how hard it is to go out alone?" The hurt in my questioner's voice and eyes was all too obvious.

This council's activities ease both situations. Sunday get-togethers help fill that day's emptiness, attending various people entertainments as a group eliminates the unpleasant awkwardness of "going alone."

A discouraged single woman whose marriage has been annulled by a Church matrimonial court process wrote the other day in deep distress: "Isn't there some group I can join? Some organization — perhaps 'Over 40, Under 50 and Still Marching' would be a good title for it — to help me meet others? Some place besides a bar, in which I can become acquainted with others in my situation?"

More One-Parent Councils with heavy Church support and active involvement by Catholic parishes might well provide an answer to her search.

* * *

Those who are still together, and happily so, nevertheless could benefit in these days from programs on parenting. Providing such informational and inspirational sessions should be high on the Church's priority list for the next decade.

At Holy Family we used for that purpose one of our "Come to the Cabaret" evenings. These twice-a-year events provide 55 couples (capacity of our renovated church hall) with an inexpensive ($6.00 per couple) Saturday night out. Seated at round tables, they sip wine, beer or soft drinks, munch on cheese and crackers, converse by candlelight and listen to approximately half-hour presentations.

This year our committee invited a local pediatrician to be the featured speaker. His topic was a broad one: "The development of children at various age levels and their parents' expectations during those periods." After a straight lecture on overall concerns involving youngsters from six months to 16 years, the audience, during a break, submitted written questions. His response to those inquiries formed the second presentation. A series of *Telespots* concluded the 8:30 to 11:30 evening.

As a sheltered celibate, I certainly learned much from the doctor's remarks about what it means to be a father or mother. Those couples, judging from the positive response, more importantly, felt better prepared for future parenting and very much reassured about the job they had done.

QUESTIONS FOR DISCUSSION

1. What advice would you give to a 16-year-old pregnant girl and her parents and to the 17-year-old father of the child and his parents? Both girl and boy are Catholic.
2. Do you think husbands and wives tend to live in our modern world more as married singles than as couples? In what way does television, work, the house, children tend to separate spouses instead of unite them? Can you suggest steps to promote "togetherness" or "coupleness" for them?

6 A Believing and Teaching People

Teachable Moments

Recently we had one of the best "kickoff" sessions we have conducted for a parental preparation program. We were beginning a yearlong period during which 70 young men and women, all at least in the seventh grade, will be preparing for the sacrament of Confirmation.

Both parents and candidates came to this 7:30 to 9:00 p.m. meeting. They heard a brief explanation of the revised approach to Confirmation, received an overview of the forthcoming activities, watched a five-minute film, listened to two recently confirmed describe their service projects, worked together on designing a cover for these journals, and joined in a concluding candle celebration.

That last event of the night was a simple ceremony of prayer, song and scripture. In addition, the candidates accepted the charge to serve persons in a special way for one year as well as to complete the other requirements. Each one came forward with a taper, lighted it from the Easter candle and returned to the pews. They promised finally to love God with their whole hearts and their neighbor as themselves.

Throughout the coming year the candidates will assemble for two large group meetings, a special community Mass, an evening of recollection, one rehearsal only and three small group sessions in homes of trained parishioners. The parents will have two other instructional gatherings, this time by themselves, which will seek to deepen their understanding of Christian initiation and the sacrament of Penance or reconciliation.

That type of program which actively involves parents in preparing their children for first reception of Eucharist and Penance together with Confirmation has become fairly standard procedure throughout the United States over the past 10 years.

These are prime teachable moments, opportunities not only to instruct the youngsters about to receive these sacraments, but also to educate the adults involved. In fact, this may prove to be the best parish adult education we have.

Inexperienced parish leaders, however, should not expect dad and mom to welcome warmly the introduction of such parent programs. Some will, but many, probably most, will initially resent the intrusion on their time or react defensively due to feelings of inadequacy about their teaching abilities.

We struggled through those obstacles for several years. Nevertheless, time, improved presentations, more efficient organization of meetings, quiet, determined leadership, realization by parents of the positive benefits—all of these factors seemed to have finally altered the climate from one of resistance or passive acceptance to general approval, even enthusiastic support of the process.

Baptism is another of those teachable moments.

Our parents of newborn infants receive a home visit from one of the staff and come to a Friday night instruction prior to the Sunday afternoon celebration of the sacrament.

Once again, not all rejoice over this new requirement ("We didn't have to come for our other babies"), but it does seem to have a beneficial effect, even for those who arrive somewhat reluctantly.

As one who performed hundreds of pre-Vatican II Baptisms which were brief, private and arranged on the spot for those who appeared without previous contact, I do know how vast a liturgical, community improvement the present practice is.

Young lovers, too, are normally well disposed for some form of instruction on Christian marriage and some type of involvement in the wedding ceremony. Priests and instructors sensitive to this can utilize these moments to lead the man and woman to a higher level of awareness concerning love and marriage.

The teachable moments programs should not exhaust the parish's adult religious education efforts, but they ought to hold first place among such activities.

To Teach as Jesus Did

The pastor or parish leadership about to evaluate a church's religious education program and set certain goals for the future must walk a delicate path and try to harmonize two norms established by the Second Vatican Council.

The *Declaration on Christian Education* states:

"Acknowledging its grave obligation to see to the moral and religious education of all its children, the Church should give special attention and help to the great number of them who are being taught in non-Catholic schools" (article 7).

"Accordingly, since the Catholic school can be of such service in developing the mission of the People of God and in promoting dialogue between the Church and the community at large to the advantage of both, it is still of vital importance even in our times" (article 8).

The parish having its own parochial school can, of course, implement within that institution a thoroughly religious education program for the young. There is ample time available, a spiritual atmosphere present, and freedom for the teachers to integrate religion into the total situation.

Moreover, with close cooperation between school and parish staffs, the thrust of the school's activities may strongly reinforce the parish's efforts. For example, teachers can encourage and facilitate pupil participation in a forthcoming Thanksgiving Day Mass or parish renewal week.

When the Catholic school is centralized, however, real concern should be given lest a certain competition arise. The school can become isolated and develop an identity of its own apart from the parishes out of which the students come. When this happens, hurt feelings result, duplicated events occur and energies are wasted.

There is no perfect resolution of that problem. Nevertheless, good communication structures between parishes and the school, as well as frequent involvement of area clergy in the school's life, may reduce those conflicts or tensions.

The parish leadership must now assign top priority to those large numbers of young people who attend public schools.

For years these latter have been second-class citizens in many parishes. Often there are overcrowded religion classes, insufficient budgets, no textbooks, well-intentioned, but inadequately trained instructors and even attitudes or principles which downgrade the public school parishioner. "Only Catholic school students are allowed to be servers." "What do you expect—they don't send the children to our school."

This situation has improved substantially in the past decade, but it does so only if parish leadership makes some hard and painful decisions which cost time, money and energy.

In our church, to illustrate, we have, over a five-year span, increased the budget from $1,000 to $15,000 for religious education, hired three sisters as parish helpers with heavy, although not exclusive, responsibilities in the catechetical field, tripled the number of CCD teachers, reduced class size from 50 to 20, negotiated with the school authorities for a better released-time schedule and built an instruction center across from the local high school.

Affirmative action programs like these can irk those who previously seemed to enjoy favored positions. Because you are doing more for public school children than before, parents of Catholic school pupils may feel you are therefore doing less now for them. We have suffered such criticism, unfair as it is (our Catholic school costs at Holy Family are $45,000 for 150 students; public school religious instruction figures are $15,000 for 740).

The parish leaders in those mixed circumstances must be extremely careful to show no partiality. The priests, particularly, are shepherds for all the children.

We have found that the clear and publicized integration of both Catholic and public school youngsters into special Sunday liturgies, e.g., the monthly children's celebration, graduation Mass, First Communion, is perhaps the most effective means of showing that we, like Jesus, love and teach equally all our boys and girls.

A Basic Beliefs Course

Parishioners generally are disposed to do something extra for God, the Church, and their own spiritual growth during the Lenten season. We sought to capitalize on that attitude one year by offering a Basic Beliefs Course throughout those six weeks.

Bulletin announcements and publicity releases for the local press indicated that the short, compact series was "for Catholics who would like to 'brush up,' for members of other Churches who are dating or planning marriage with a Catholic and have questions, and for all those who would like to investigate Catholic beliefs and practice without any obligation."

A surprisingly large number of people responded (average attendance, 42). Moreover, their intense interest for the entire double-lecture, two-hour Monday night sessions quickly convinced me we had discovered a program much needed at the present moment.

We used two basic texts, both relatively inexpensive paperbacks: *Christ Among Us* by Paulist Father Anthony J. Wilhelm and the very popular *Good News for Modern Man*.

The course followed in the main a lecture format, but with some time for questions and answers and a sprinkling of various audiovisuals to supplement the verbal and chalkboard presentations.

These topic titles for the six evenings should give readers an idea of the content: "God, God's Book, God's People"; "Jesus Christ, His Life and His Church"; "The Catholic Church"; "Worship and the World"; "Sin and Forgiveness, Love and Sickness"; "The Christian Life Here and Hereafter."

A legal-size, mimeographed sheet of paper listed essential facts about the series and the course outline. It also indictated the pertinent chapters in both Wilhelm's text and *Good News for Modern Man*.

Priests and religious educators, anxious to move Roman Catholics along the renewal path of Vatican II, sometimes may forget that the ordinary lay person still wonders about and asks very rudimentary religious questions like these which follow.

How do we know there is a God? Did Jesus have brothers and sisters? What is a cardinal? A monsignor? Are Catholics excommunicated when they get a divorce? May Protestants be godparents for a Baptism? What about priests in politics?

Our participants raised these inquiries and many more. Most were Catholics seeking to update themselves and settle some issues about the changing Church which have troubled them. About a dozen, however, either had no church affiliation or tenuously belonged to different Protestant congregations. Half of these became members of the Catholic Church after completion of the course.

Smooth and effective introduction of the revised rite for Penance will require over the next decade continued instruction of the type given in our Basic Beliefs Course. If believers are to feel comfortable with new provisions and benefit from them, they must know not only what to do, but why.

Consider, for example, the extension of hands over a penitent; the 10 suggested acts of contrition; the reading of scripture by penitent, priest or both; the assignment and acceptance of personal, creative acts of satisfaction complementing or replacing traditional Our Fathers and Hail Marys; communal services with and without absolution; prayerful dialogue between confessor and sinner; the face-to-face encounters in rooms of reconciliation rather than anonymous exchanges in traditional boxes.

Parish Personal Enrichment Week

Father Camillus Barth is a 69-year-old, bald, energetic Passionist missionary preacher. For 40 years he has, like St. Paul, been preaching. He lives at a monastery in West Springfield, Massachusetts, but his regular operating bases are various rectories throughout the United States.

I met him, liked the creative, contemporary approach he favored in presenting traditional Christian good news concepts and asked him to spend a week with us. Parishioners had not experienced a "mission" in over a decade and our staff felt this might prove an excellent preparation for the then approaching Holy Year. The response exceeded everyone's most optimistic expectations.

The Passionists know that careful preparation on the local level is the key to a successful parish retreat. To facilitate this, they send an advance man who supplies host personnel with posters, data and suggested steps for proper publicity. In addition, they request detailed information about the nature of the community—number of families, age breakdown, yearly Baptisms, marriages and funerals, Mass schedule, general spiritual needs, etc.

We termed the retreat a "Personal Enrichment Week" rather than a mission and in the homily two weeks beforehand indicated as its purpose the goals of renewal and reconciliation.

A press release for the local newspapers began in this way:

"Have the problems and complexities of modern-day life confused or discouraged you? Do you find the mystery of life itself baffling? How do you view yourself, as a somebody or a nobody?

"Is your faith in God stronger or weaker than it was a few years ago? Does prayer help you cope with your personal life? Have you given up praying?

"Is religion a comfort for you, an obligation, or something no longer of value? Are you a sinner anxious for God's forgiveness, afraid to ask or not sure you know how? Do you need help with some personal decisions about the future?

"If any of these questions strike home, you might consider participating in the Personal Enrichment Week, Nov. 3-8 at Holy Family Church in Fulton."

We followed up that announcement story one week later with a photograph of staff members preparing for the week and a paid advertisement professionally designed by an agency operated by a Holy Family parishioner.

During the seed-sowing sermon preceding Father Camillus' arrival, we asked our people to pray for God's blessing on this week (with a special plea directed toward the very young children), to make a sacrifice each day on its behalf, and to act as spiritual missionaries by inviting someone who could benefit from the experience.

Father Barth opened the Personal Enrichment Week by preaching at all the Sunday Masses. Obviously aware of the essential importance of these words, he spoke at length (20 minutes) and captivated the congregations with his wit, enthusiasm, dynamic style and powerful message.

Sunday night, however, was the acid test. Would they return? Over 500 did, listened attentively and even applauded at one point.

The next day they came back, and the next, and the next until Friday's closing. Every morning we averaged 125 for the 9:15 Mass and conference; 500 to 600 participated in the evening's 7:30 repeated service.

Volunteers served coffee and cookies downstairs after each session with family bibles and religious articles available for purchase.

Father Camillus, assisted by one of us, heard confessions for lengthy periods after the daily presentations. A wife spoke to me with grateful tears at the week's conclusion, overjoyed that her husband had found the desire and courage to approach a priest and receive this sacrament after an absence of many years. I am sure he was not the only one so moved.

There were no collections during the series except on the last day when the Passionist made a brief, low-key appeal. Concerned priests should be reassured to learn that the amount realized nicely covered not only a generous stipend for his community and for him, but also the expenses involved in this week.

The Church, of course, enriches such retreats or missions with special indulgences. I am also convinced the Holy Spirit operates in unique ways during these periods of prayer, preaching and reflection. Certainly for the people of Holy Family, those were days of deep renewal and peaceful reconciliation.

Handing Down Our Heritage

Msgr. Ray Teller and his co-workers in the religious education office for the Archdiocese of Philadelphia believe it is one thing to talk about preaching the gospel and quite another actually to do it. Seeking to translate such thought and talk into actions and projects, they organized a pilot "Evangelization Program" designed "for everyone interested in the Catholic Church and her teachings." The basic model was followed from October-December in 25 centers of the Philadelphia area.

Over 1,400 persons registered for the course and participated in these sessions, a turnout clearly indicating that evangelization of this nature fulfills a need for many individuals in contemporary society. The planners took as their guiding principle a definition from the Synod of Bishops on the Evangelization of the Modern World: "Evangelization is the activity whereby the gospel is proclaimed and explained, and whereby living faith is awakened in non-Christians."

The series presented a complete survey of Catholic teaching achieved through a one night each week, one-and-one-half-hour session for 11 weeks. Individual classes did not follow a straight lecture, then question and answer pattern. Instead, the program attempted to develop an experiential approach, modeling this example of Christ:

"In teaching, Jesus did not ordinarily present theological

A Believing and Teaching People

formulations to be memorized, but rather he shared a religious experience. He encouraged dialogue by asking questions (e.g., "Who do men say that I am?"). He also listened and allowed time for prayer and reflection. Moreover, in a fascinating way, he celebrated the presence of God." Thus every evening included presentation of the theme, audiovisual materials, group discussion and a related experience activity.

For example, Lesson 10, "We are a prayerful people who worship," contained a lecture on prayer and worship, then audiovisuals explaining the "Our Father" and "The Rosary Story." Discussion followed on these questions: Why do we say that breathing to the body is what prayer is to the soul? What is charismatic prayer? Is it better to pray with others or to pray alone? Do memorized formulas have value in prayer? How do we improve attention and awareness in prayer?

The session concluded with Benediction or, if that was not possible, the rosary, stations of the cross or some other recognized devotion. Other evenings ended with similar activities for and by participants: a bible service, shared prayer, renewal of baptismal promises, celebration of the Eucharist, a value clarification exercise, some social action (e.g., bringing an elderly or neglected person to the session), a penitential service.

These topic or theme titles indicate the course's subject matter: "Who We Are and God," "The Great Book With God's Message," "Wonder at the Mystery of God," "God-Man Among Us," "The Family That Is the Church," "Signs in Which We Meet God," "One Bread Makes Us One Body," "Moral Life of a Christian," "Encounter With a Forgiving Christ," "We Are a Prayerful People Who Worship," "Living Daily the Christian Life."

The intricacies of Old Testament history, including matters like the Yahwist and Elohist traditions, together with the riches of the Church's past and present, cannot be absorbed in a single sitting, or in 11 for that matter. But a program like the Philadelphia series does give those interested a fine initiation into our rich heritage.

Msgr. Teller, as a result of the pilot project, argues convincingly that a survey course of this nature ought to be offered each year in every parish.

Priests' Pursuit of Wisdom

Msgr. Charles Eckermann serves as principal of Bishop Ludden High School in Syracuse, New York, but last fall he instead went back to school from September 22 to November 14. Msgr. Eckermann joined two dozen priests from the other dioceses of New York state for a Provincial Priests' Institute held at St. Joseph's Seminary in Dunwoodie.

These clergymen, some young, but most ordained at least 15 years ago, came for an academic retooling program, a two-month period of lectures, reading, prayer and recreation. They hoped, in the process, to catch up on theological developments which have taken place within the Church since Vatican II. The participants in the beginning probably came for a variety of reasons—perhaps in response to their bishops' request, perhaps simply to get away from duties back home, perhaps as an attempt to feel more comfortable with the thrust of current theology, perhaps to prepare themselves (as Msgr. Eckermann did) for future responsibilities as pastors of parishes.

But I heard nothing but praise for the institute from the priests during my overnight visit to that New York seminary. There was no restlessness among them, no anxiety about matters back in the diocese, no impatient desire to get back "on the firing line." Not that these two months were given over solely to leisure and rest. On the contrary, the participants followed a crammed, seven-day-a-week schedule, with only intermittent days, afternoons or evenings free.

The format on the day of my presentation was typical. Following common recitation of morning prayer from the breviary, the priests went to a lecture from 9:15-11:15 (with coffee break) by Father John O'Grady of Albany on St. John's Gospel. They concelebrated Mass at 11:40, lunched, then spent some time in rest or recreation.

In the middle or late afternoon they were in their rooms and at their desks reading one of the many texts recommended by the 40 professors who teach in the program. After one-two hours of this, they gathered for presupper socializing, dinner and a brief after-meal walk.

When night prayer had been completed, they sat down in the classroom ready for my two-hour presentation on "Parish Liturgy." Some continued their reading afterwards, but with that kind of schedule most turned out lights quite early and prepared for another similar calendar of events the next day.

Msgr. Eckermann studied at the North American College in Rome prior to his ordination about 20 years ago, worked for a period in the parish ministry, taught at Catholic schools, worked on statewide educational committees and has directed Bishop Ludden for some time. With such a variety of posts and responsibilities, he has found it a necessity to keep informed on Church developments. However, the Syracuse priest still observed: "I didn't realize just how much has happened and how much has passed me by in 10 years, especially in the study of scripture."

The board of directors, composed of bishops and three priests from the province, hope this pilot program will help fill that kind of vacuum, renew old study habits and spiritually rejuvenate priests of the state. It seems the project is succeeding and I think these individual priests will return much wiser and better equipped to serve their people.

Those priests and participants of future institutes would do well to start by reading the book of Proverbs and Sirach. These Old Testament texts invite persons to pursue wisdom, the general purpose of that New York State Priests' Institute.

QUESTIONS FOR DISCUSSION

1. If, in your parish, some young people attend Catholic schools and others, public institutions of learning, discuss the relationships between them. How can the parish relate more closely to a centralized Catholic elementary or secondary school? What programs or efforts could be made to bind all the young people together, those in Catholic schools and those in secular institutions?

2. Unless we are willing to change, no learning is possible. Sometimes we refuse really to listen because deep down we fear that what will be said may force us to alter our thinking or living. Discuss and give examples, such as in the relationship between men and women or concerning change within the Church.

7 A Caring People

The Mind, Yes; the Heart, No

On a Sunday afternoon soon after publication of the new rite for anointing the sick, I stopped for a visit at the home of an ailing parishioner. He was seriously ill, but not critical at that point and certainly in no imminent danger of death.

We had talked for 15 minutes or so when I inquired if he would like to be anointed. The sudden change in his expression really surprised me. Our conversation stopped, his jaw tightened and he looked with a quiet grimness off into the distance.

His wife broke the silence and mentioned homilies we had given on previous Sundays about the healing power of this sacrament. The children repeated similar thoughts, ideas they had absorbed at the local Catholic schools. But to no avail. For the moment this notion of receiving "last rites" overwhelmed him and I dropped the subject.

I should not have been so stunned by his reaction.

A few words from the pulpit, a paragraph or two in the bulletin, a magazine article may successfully explain some new change in the Church and gain our mental acceptance. But moving our hearts to accept the innovation is quite a different process, a much harder and longer one.

Our sick parishioner knew all about the revised approach

to this sacrament; he had listened to those sermons, glanced at the bulletins, read the article. But a near half century of living and learning about the priest giving "last rites" leaves deep impressions within a person's being and attitudes formed over so many years are not altered immediately. His heart for the present just wouldn't or couldn't go along with this change.

In a way, Catholics have been taught and trained too well. Our thorough earlier formation has placed some obstacles in the path of renewal. It often makes painfully difficult approval of a new development even when this reform is highly desirable, carefully introduced and strongly supported by papal authority.

We can cite several other illustrations of this clash between what the head grasps and the heart will accept.

Consider, for example, large, thick brown altar breads in place of tiny, thin, white Communion wafers. There are several cogent reasons why the former should be used; but many Catholic Christians rebel against their insertion within Mass.

I feel guilty, some will say, chewing those larger particles. We were told never to do so. Others will recall instruction which linked the holiness and purity of Jesus with the whiteness of the host.

They may nod in agreement when these points are explained; but in practice, at least for a long time, their hearts, their feelings will say no.

Lay ministers of Holy Communion are another instance. After decades of reminders that only the sacred hands of a priest may touch the host, we should expect hesitant acceptance or even hostile rejection of a development in which relatives, friends and neighbors have suddenly been granted this privilege.

Once again, critics may acknowledge the validity of all

historical and doctrinal arguments supporting this move. But their feelings and their hearts will not follow what their heads dictate.

A final example—applause in church. This activity runs sharply counter to past instruction which identified reverence with silence. One may lecture in detail about celebration, spontaneity and clapping as a natural expression of inner joy or approval. The audience may intellectually assent to such a presentation. I doubt, however, if every listener would feel comfortable applauding on the next occasion when it occurs during worship.

By a Dying Person's Bedside

Deathly ill persons often hear and understand more than visitors realize.

Ken Herbert, a pseudonym for an elderly, dying man in our community, personally has underscored this truth I was taught in my seminary days.

I first met Mr. Herbert only a few weeks ago, but in that short time I have become extremely close to this noble individual.

Our initial encounters came in the local hospital where doctors and nurses were trying with oxygen tubes to pour new life into his diseased lungs. A Catholic relative asked me to visit him, to pray over a man whose past religious background was uncertain and present practice, minimal. I did so gladly, but the visits were short, the prayers brief and, in his weakened condition, I judged he scarcely grasped who I was or what I did.

Mr. Herbert's state soon improved slightly, enough at least to send him home.

Several days later a son-in-law left a message at the

rectory that the old man was calling for me. I stopped in the evening at his house, not expecting to do much more than show by my presence and prayers some interest and concern.

Ken's verbal communications now were but painful, gasping whispers uttered at lengthy intervals.

To my surprise, he recognized my voice and touch and to my shock, said he had, since teenage days, always wanted to be a Catholic. A few simple questions indicated this was not the confused wish of a dying person, but the lifelong desire of an individual near death.

I conditionally baptized him, anointed forehead and hands with oil of the sick, bestowed the apostolic blessing and spoke a few final prayers in his ear.

Afterwards he slowly responded: "Thank you very . . . very . . . very . . . much."

Within days Mr. Herbert returned to the hospital and the specialized care it offers.

After confessions last Saturday night I made my customary evening rounds at the hospital. As I walked into Ken's room he spoke a word of recognition despite his rapidly failing health and vision.

We prayed together using the new "Rite of Anointing and Pastoral Care of the Sick."

"Father . . . would you say . . . that prayer . . . about green pastures?"

"Of course, Ken . . . 'The Lord is my shepherd; I shall not want. In green pastures he gives me repose. . . .' "

"That's . . . such . . . a . . . beautiful . . . prayer . . ."

"Ken, I am going to whisper a few brief phrases from the bible into your ear. All right?"

He nodded approval and closed his eyes.

"What can come between us and the love of Christ? . . . What can come between us and the love of Christ?"

"Nothing . . . nothing, Father."

This marvelous, unsolicited response stunned me and almost brought tears to my eyes.

"We shall see God as he really is . . . We shall see God as he really is . . . We shall see God as he really is . . ."

"Father . . . how wonderful . . . it will be . . . when I kneel . . . before him . . . in heaven."

Before leaving, I gently stroked his hand for a few moments only to have him lift my fingers to his lips and kiss them.

I wrote these words a couple of days later at 39,000 feet en route to Seattle and a conference for priests on the care of sick persons. Ken Herbert may have, by that time, already begun his journey to heaven. But he was with me at those talks and I hope in my memory for years to come.

Discovering an Old Man's Life

I only knew Edward "Babe" Gschwender during the final three years of his life—from the time of our introduction shortly after my arrival at Holy Family until his death.

With a relatively large parish like ours, a priest's knowledge of his people varies greatly. Some persons are involved in many activities and through those frequent contacts, we learn not only their names, but where they live, who is close to them, what are their joys and hopes, their griefs and anxieties.

Other less active, yet regular Sunday worshipers become known by name and are familiar faces in their customary spots at church. Our understanding of them, however, often stops on that surface level until some particular event (First Communion, for example) or crisis (sickness, family trouble, death) brings us into closer contact.

For me, Babe and his wife, Bernardine, fell into that second category.

Every Sunday I saw them in the back pew, left side; within a year or two I finally got their first names clearly in my mind; on one occasion, I transmitted a message to them from a congressman friend met on an airplane; I also made a brief afternoon census visit to the home. But that was all—a friendly, concerned, interested, yet superficial acquaintanceship.

Babe had retired prior to my appointment and, at 70, seemed rather feeble, in precarious health, and not able to participate much in parish life.

Their several months' absence from that customary back pew location eventually began to dawn on me, but, pressed by other matters, I did not investigate the reason behind it. Finally, as is often the case, a friend left a message about Mr. Gschwender's deteriorating condition.

I stopped at the house one stormy night, learned of the illness and prayed for Babe. Shortly thereafter he entered our local hospital.

My partner in the parish anointed him and gave him viaticum; our two sisters in pastoral ministry visited the ailing man on several occasions; I dropped in on three or four occasions for a few words, imposed hands on his cold, bald head and offered a brief prayer.

The day before he died, in response to my blessing, Babe raised his right arm, burdened with IV tubes and anchoring board, crossed himself and whispered a "Thank you, Father."

I didn't really know Mr. Gschwender, however, until some hours after he died. That night (snowy, as on the previous occasion), I spent an hour with Bernardine and her only son in their home. They brought out a scrapbook of clippings about Babe—about his retirement party, about a testimonial banquet honoring the volunteer work he did in the community, about earlier days as a basketball star.

Now the sickly old man I knew became the popular

personnel manager at a local factory, the energetic founder of a recreational hall, the conscientious promoter of an area blood bank. Here was a man who gave an estimated 20 gallons of blood during his lifetime—for believers and unbelievers, for Catholics and Protestants, for friends and for strangers. Here I discovered an individual who spent many sleepless nights seeking donors with special-type plasma for critically ill patients.

With a grasp of that background, the funeral homily became much more personal and the gospel text chosen, better suited to the situation.

"He who feeds on my flesh and drinks my blood has life eternal, and I will raise him up on the last day."

I wonder how many other elderly persons in my nearly 20 years of ministry there were whose full lives never became evident to me until after their deaths or perhaps not at all.

Preparing for the Risen Lord

Elizabeth Ann Garrett Schermerhorn was a woman with deep faith and a sharp tongue, a person of blunt honesty and great loyalty to the Church. She did not care for many of the changes introduced in her parish since Vatican II. More than once Betty vented to me in no uncertain terms these hostile feelings about innovations such as lay ministers of Communion and nuns without habits or the disappearance of traditional devotions and proper respect or the failure of modern priests to give the sick suitable attention.

But this strong-willed 54-year-old wife and mother would at the end of a tirade then smile impishly or sheepishly and remark: "Well, the old grouch is at it again."

About three years ago Elizabeth Ann's world, and the world of her husband and three teenage children, turned upside down. After weeks of persistent, but inexplicable pain, she went to a specialist in Syracuse for extensive tests and a diagnosis.

The verdict was one word—a term with fatal connotations which every American dreads to hear.

During the months which followed there were the typical developments: various drugs and therapy treatments, confinement at home and periods of hospitalization, prayer and worry, discomfort and discouragement. At one point, early in the illness, I asked if she would like to be anointed. There was no response, only a grey look, downcast eyes and tightened lips. Betty's husband encouraged reception of this sacrament, but for the moment that ritual was for her "last rites," not "anointing of the sick" and she could not then quite cope with thoughts of death and dying.

However, six months later she consented to the ritual and in fact received this healing sacrament several times before her death in January of our bicentennial year.

While a relatively imminent final passage from this life to a heavenly home was really anticipated from the day her diagnosis became known, the last hours came upon the family in sudden fashion. A massive internal hemorrhage sent Betty by ambulance to Upstate Hospital's emergency room at 4:30 one winter afternoon.

The end came at 11:00 p.m., but preceded by a beautiful, loving, faith-filled preparation for her meeting with the Risen Lord.

Elizabeth Ann's husband, Walt, was there; so, too, were her son, two daughters, parish priest and three friends. The nurses kept close watch and one supported Betty's back lovingly for two straight hours.

Every 10 or 15 minutes the priest bent over and whispered short biblical prayers into her ear.

"Jesus, thy will be done."

A Caring People

"Mother Seton, pray for me."
"Into your hands, O Lord, I commend my spirit."
"My Lord and my God."
"We shall know him as he really is."

The children held her hands, Walt stroked her forehead. Every now and then Betty opened her eyes or spoke a few words, playing the grouch role even at that point of life. The last gesture she made under her own steam was a sign of the cross.

We all withdrew around 11:00 p.m. to allow the nurses to change a dressing on the desperately ill woman. The delay seemed ominously long to me, when a nurse stepped out and softly said to Walt: "She's gone."

There were abundant tears at Betty's funeral, but rich support from the Church's liturgy. Several priests concelebrated the Mass, high school classmates proclaimed the readings, a Christian Brother who taught Walt led the congregation in a prayer of the faithful, the music spoke movingly of the Resurrection.

The entire family brought gifts forward at presentation time: bread, wine and symbols of Betty's life—her wedding band, her mother's ring with the children's birthstones on it, a golden rosary and a relic of Mother Seton. St. Elizabeth Ann Seton had a message for the Schermerhorn family. It was the same one she gave to her own spiritual children when the first American saint approached death.

In a way she and Betty offered the three motherless youngsters this charge: "Be children of the Church."

To the empty, stunned, mourning husband, they both urged him to pray: "May the most just, the most high, and the most amiable will of God be accomplished forever."

Stages of Dying

"Who are those urging us to accept death? They are individuals programmed by the Puritan old world of guilt and punishment to regard suffering and death as necessities. In desperation they hold onto fantasies of life after death.

"But a new consciousness is emerging, relatively free of Puritan guilt, vigorous and life-oriented. To this liberated consciousness death is an end. There is no paradise, no heaven, hell or reincarnated life. Death, therefore, is a greater tragedy now than ever before."

So wrote F. M. Esfandiary in "Sorry, We're Here for Eternity," an essay appearing in the September 24, 1974, issue of the *New York Times*.

The author, apparently, takes a dim view of Dr. Elisabeth Kubler-Ross, the medical director of the Family Service and Mental Health Center of South Cook County, Ill. Physician-psychiatrist Mrs. Kubler-Ross has become famous through her book, *On Death and Dying* (Collier Books, 866 Third Avenue, New York, 10022).

That enormously popular and helpful paperback details her work with terminally sick patients in Chicago and summarizes "what the dying have to teach doctors, nurses, clergy and their own families." In it she develops the now familiar five stages deathly ill persons generally pass through in their last days and hours. The final one is acceptance, an attitude Esfandiary finds objectionable.

Since we all must face our own personal deaths sooner or later and will also in the course of a lifetime suffer those final moments with at least several individuals dear to us, the advantage of everyone having a familiarity with these stages should be obvious. Incidentally, people close to the dying tend likewise to experience some or all of the inner feelings involved with those five steps.

First stage: denial and isolation. Death so frightens and overwhelms most of us that in the beginning we either deny its reality and possibility or withdraw temporarily from others to sort the matter out in our minds.

We look to doctors, nurses, clergy, relatives and friends to support the denial. "I feel better today." "The doctor says I should be home soon." "Don't you think I am improving?" During this period we are consciously and unconsciously trying to build up the courage required to cope with our dreaded future.

Second stage: anger. "Why is this happening to me?" "How could God do such a thing? I have always been a good person." "Why not him or her?" That envy, resentment, bitter feeling, rage stems from our inability to handle or change a painful situation.

The frustration strikes out at innocent victims, once again the physician, nursing staff, priest, relatives, friends. "Why don't you do something about this?" "How come you haven't been here more often?" Those attacked need great patience in these moments and the wisdom not to take personally that misplaced anger.

Third stage: bargaining. The patient (or person near to the dying individual) occasionally will make a bargain, normally kept secret, for an extension of life, usually for a specified period. "I will do such and such, if I can be spared until my daughter's wedding."

Fourth stage: depression. A sadness floods the dying person over the loss of past valued objects—family, job, finances, positions, etc.—and the impending separation which comes with death.

"Don't be sad" is a natural, but not wise way of trying to comfort the depressed patient. Instead, those close to the individual would do well to let him or her express that sorrow.

Later, the dying person may speak less about the losses and simply remain silently sad. In those hours the gentle stroking of hand or forehead is often the best method of offering comfort and support.

Stage five: acceptance. Tired and weak, requiring much sleep and rest, at peace, not bothered by the outside world or interested in visitors, communicating normally in nonverbal ways, the dying person has not given up, but rather senses the pain is over, the struggle finished and waits with resignation and acceptance for the final long journey.

Those nearest the dying individual often need more assistance now than does the terminally ill person.

It should be evident to readers how a strong faith in the Christian message, promising life forever, can make the passage from stage one to stage five easier and swifter.

QUESTIONS FOR DISCUSSION

1. Describe how you felt visiting a sick person, especially a terminally ill friend or relative. Would you be comfortable making the sign of the cross on that individual's forehead or reciting short scriptural passages into his or her ear?
2. Read through again the five stages of dying and share with the group an incident or several situations in which you or someone else experienced one or more of those attitudes and feelings.

SECTION III

THE LARGER CHURCH AND A WIDER VISION

8 The Bishop-- A Leader of Many

Bishop Topel Speaks on Penance

Bishop Bernard Topel of Spokane has become somewhat nationally famous in recent years. His personal example of prayerfulness and commitment to a simple life-style have won the admiration of many in the Church, especially among those who favor a change in the customary manner bishops live and act.

At the same time, more traditional-oriented Catholics may feel less comfortable and enthusiastic about a shepherd who sells the episcopal mansion and moves into a modest apartment with lower-income neighbors, who cultivates his own garden and cooks his own food, who wants to free himself from the chancery desk and mix with people, who shows a sympathy for those in trouble with the law.

The diocesan liturgical commission members from throughout the United States who worshiped with Bishop Topel in Spokane at Our Lady of Lourdes Cathedral during an annual conference fall into both categories. Most probably consider themselves progressives, anxious for change and heavily supportive of Bishop Topel's approach. The minority would likely judge themselves traditionalists, more cautious about change, impressed, but not excited by Bishop Topel's style of leadership.

The sheer example of this bishop, however, commands

The Bishop: A Leader of Many

respect whatever your viewpoint and thus when he began the homily both groups of participants listened intently. In his lengthy talk, Bishop Topel strongly urged frequent use of the sacrament of Penance (even suggesting a weekly confession of sins). It seemed a strange twist of roles.

That was hardly the message most "progressives" expected. Some of them, I know, responded negatively to his message even though they acknowledged the apparent holiness of the preacher. On the other hand, "traditionalists" seemed pleasantly surprised and endorsed with enthusiasm the thrust of that homily.

Bishop Topel cited the teaching of St. Francis de Sales, the encyclical by Pius XII on the Mystical Body of Christ and the Liturgy Constitution from Vatican II in support of his position.

Pope Pius in that papal document listed these benefits from frequent reception of Penance:

"By it genuine self-knowledge is increased, Christian humility is developed, bad habits are corrected, spiritual neglect and tepidity are countered, the conscience is purified, the will is strengthened, salutary self-control is obtained, and an increase of grace is secured by the very fact that the sacrament is received."

Spokane's shepherd offered his own life as a case in point. Since he sought the assistance of a regular spiritual director and began (or renewed) the practice of frequent confession, his concept of the episcopacy has changed. In fact, he maintains that those very socially aware actions for which progressives applaud him developed as a result of the sensitivity gained through these weekly (or more often?) receptions of Penance.

Bishop Topel, who celebrates the Eucharist in warm, relaxed, friendly fashion with occasional touches of humor, revealed three faults he presently is seeking to overcome and the corresponding virtues he is trying to develop: the failure to love others as Christ does, the lack of gratitude for God's many gifts, and the absence of a proper trust in the Lord.

To objectors who argue, "You don't have to go to confession," the bishop counters, "You don't have to receive Holy Communion either."

To critics who claim they get nothing out of this sacrament, Bishop Topel responds, "It is your own fault because you haven't put enough into it."

Death Comes for the Archbishop

A cabdriver in the Twin Cities told me, several weeks later, just how impressive and moving he found the two-hour, televised funeral of Archbishop Leo Byrne, Coadjutor of St. Paul-Minneapolis.

Four or five months afterwards I heard similar comments, this time from an individual who personally participated in the liturgy itself, youthful Bishop Bernard Law of the Springfield-Cape Girardeau Diocese in Missouri.

Bishop Law, like all of us, especially those in leadership positions, finds himself caught between conflicting demands. He constantly must make priority judgments as to the allocations of his limited time and energy. How much of my life, he inquires, should be given to the chancery office, to visiting throughout our diocese, to statewide concerns, to national meetings, to ecumenical activities, to community social action committees?

Traveling to Minnesota for the Christian burial of a brother bishop who had died suddenly, unexpectedly, of a heart attack held a high place on that priority list. With some 65 other bishops, he felt his presence there would prove of some comfort to the people of this archdiocese who had lost their shepherd.

It took nearly a half hour for all those prelates and over 1,000 priests to process into the Twin Cities Cathedral. The local liturgy planners under the direction of Auxiliary Bishop Raymond Lucker, anticipated that delay and employed the time wisely.

They devised a litany of death patterned after the familiar general intercessions or prayer of the faithful to accompany this slow-moving procession. The petitions, centering around the sorrowing church of St. Paul-Minneapolis, were chanted according to the Byzantine melody, but without any musical accompaniment. A period of silence followed each intention, broken only by the occasional beat of muffled drums (as in the burial service for a president) and the rustle of processing clergy.

Unfortunately, in our enthusiasm to stress the Resurrection element in a Christian funeral liturgy, we sometimes ignore or dismiss too lightly the sadness, grief and pain felt by mourners. That was not the case in St. Paul.

The hope, serenity and peace so richly present in a Christian's burial service came soon enough. A thunderous pre-Gospel Alleluia with brass support, an enormous choir and congregational singing told in convincing tones to everyone present and watching that there is more than sorrow and a crushing finality when a follower of Christ dies.

At the presentation of gifts, four signs of Archbishop Byrne's life were brought forward with great solemnity. The meaning of each was explained in the participation leaflet distributed to the congregation beforehand. That eliminated the need for comments within the ceremony itself and allowed the symbols to speak their own powerful message.

First, servers carried in majestic fashion the white, decorated funeral pall and draped it over the Archbishop's casket. This, his greatest dignity: being a Christian, a follower of Jesus, a person destined by the Lord for eternal life.

Next, a stole, symbolic of his priesthood begun some 40 years earlier.

Third, the miter placed on his head when he became a bishop.

Finally, the crozier, the shepherd's crook, the staff, indicative of his responsibility over those thousands in Minnesota who had benefited from his leadership while he lived and now watched as the Christian community sent him home for his reward in the Father's everlasting house.

A Bishop Who Loves His People

Sometimes only the sudden snuffing out of innocent persons' lives will bring the general population to a realization of some evil which needs removal from their midst. For example, while the number of abortions remains at a discouragingly astronomical level, it seems that many, including certain physicians, have in view of what has happened begun to withdraw their previously unqualified support for the procedure. Surely any young (or old) person viewing those standard slides of an aborted fetus used in the prolife, antiabortion campaign must entertain second thoughts about the issue.

The tragic bombing deaths in 1964 of four girls in the 16th Street Baptist Church of Birmingham had such an effect upon the people of that city in Alabama. They had heard before from an eloquent preacher (Dr. Martin Luther King's famous "Letter from a Birmingham Jail") about the need in their city for mutual love, respect and acceptance despite racial differences. But apparently it took the horrible event of four innocent young persons losing their lives so needlessly to open the eyes of Birmingham and all of Alabama.

Bishop Joseph Vath, the 55-year-old, first shepherd of the new Birmingham Diocese, believes this to be the case. He cites as his proof a youth Mass he offered in 1974, 10 years after the bombing incident. During that liturgy, black and white children sang, prayed, worshiped together in an obvious display of great Christian love and concern for one another.

This youth Mass was one of the many activities during his "Deanery Live-ins." Seven times a year Bishop Vath leaves the chancery, becomes unavailable except for dire emergencies and spends a week in a deanery of the diocese. The bishop does so to show that as shepherd he knows, loves and cares about his people, appreciates their support, and needs them for the work of the Church.

Individuals in the process obviously come to feel they are needed and wanted; they also sense better their own dignity and importance.

In the smaller deaneries, Bishop Vath is able to visit each parish every year; in the larger sections, that visitation extends over a few years before he can cover all the parishes. The Bishop meets with deanery priests of a specific region beforehand and determines for them where his presence would be most beneficial—a school, prison, parish council, nursing home, etc. They then arrange a series of activities for him during the weeklong stay in that particular area.

The following incidents illustrate the nature of these deanery live-ins:

- Talking during a day in the local prison with the inmates, bringing Communion to five of them and discussing penal reform with the criminal judges.

- Visiting various factories.

- Spending four hours in the wilderness of a virgin forest with the pastor of the parish in which the preserve is located. There he was able to take a cup and dip into the clean, pure waters of a stream which farther south in his diocese becomes a green, polluted river.

- Calling upon the residents of nursing homes, praying with them, offering these often forgotten individuals the consolation of the faith.
- Sitting down with each priest, especially those in separated missions, for a two- to three-hour easy, informal talk about his needs, his ministry and his parish.

Bishop Vath views these live-ins as excellent opportunities for the diocesan shepherd to be just that—a shepherd—a pastor who is concerned and cares about all the members of his flock. It helps him convey to people of the Birmingham Diocese that each person, however young or old, is important and has value.

The Bishop as Leader

One of our more gifted and prolific Catholic writers in the United States has, over the past months, frequently and bitterly decried the lack of leadership given at the present time by the American bishops. This critic, however, has not so often or so clearly delineated the meaning of true leadership or the type of leaders desired. That remains a more difficult, a more complex task.

Strong episcopal leaders are heroes and courageous prophets to those who agree with their views; they are reactionaries and unenlightened dictators to those who oppose their decisions. Bishop Maher of San Diego, for example, by refusing Communion to persons active in organizations which endorse abortion, has become an instant hero to those in the right-to-life movement and a hated enemy to those in the NOW organization.

Episcopal leaders who follow Cardinal Suenens' recommendations and seek to unite the entire diocese suffer the wrath of both those who wish to stay behind and those who wish to run ahead. Too fast for some, too slow for others, that bishop likewise may be called a compromiser, a wishy-washy person, a man without leadership abilities. Quite the contrary, his reconciling ways can indicate he has a unique talent for moving the entire community ahead at a steady, gradual pace.

Bishops who observe a *laissez-faire,* "he rules best, who rules least," disposed-to-overlook approach will win the support and admiration of many. Others, however, will object to this style and claim he fails to uphold true values and lends tacit approval to erroneous opinions and activities.

I am not sure how to categorize Bishop Paul Donovan of the recently formed diocese of Kalamazoo, Michigan. However, he certainly has given an example of leadership in his manner of moving about the area, meeting constantly with people and calling for shared responsibility in the pastoral decision process.

Parishioners of St. Catherine's Church in Portage experienced Bishop Donovan's giving presence over an entire weekend.

He lunched Saturday noon with the total staff (priests, sisters, etc.) and in the afternoon brought Holy Communion to six or seven parishioners confined at home because of illness.

Later in the day he celebrated the sacrament of Penance (our new expression for "hearing confessions") from 5 to 6 and 8 to 9, offered the anticipated evening Mass and preached at that liturgy.

The next day the relatively young bishop preached at the three Sunday Masses and shared coffee and doughnuts afterwards with parishioners. The pastor estimates he shook hands and greeted 75 percent of St. Catherine's people during these social hours.

Bishop Donovan completed his weekend at St. Catherine's by lunching with parish council members and their spouses, sitting through the regular meeting as an observer and then visiting informally with them at the session's termination.

Leadership entails more than shaking hands and greeting people. But a bishop who moves around, observes carefully and listens intently will be in a much better position to make forward-thinking, wise decisions and to serve as an inspiring leader for all.

Selecting a New Bishop

"He who governs all should be selected by all."

"It comes from divine authority that a bishop be chosen in the presence of all the people before the eyes of all, and that he be approved as worthy and fit by public judgment and testimony."

Do these quotes sound like the brash assertions of angry liberals who maintain a bishop today ought to be elected by the people? They are in fact words attributed to Pope Gregory the Great and St. Cyprian. Those leaders of the Church centuries ago apparently felt the general populace's voice would help insure the choice of a Christlike shepherd.

This question of how a new bishop is or should be selected recently became a very practical concern and a matter of importance for people in our diocese. A bishop who celebrates his 75th birthday must, according to Church regulations, submit a formal resignation sometime during the next year. When and if that action is accepted by the Holy Father, a new shepherd is appointed to the diocese. That was the situation recently in our diocese and the Bishop's Senate of Priests has been anxious to offer those responsible for that selection its ideas about the present state and the future needs of our diocese as well as a general profile of the desirable qualities in the bishop who ultimately will succeed.

To achieve that goal, the Senate appointed a committee of representative priests, religious and lay persons who were joined by a personal delegate of the bishop. This highly qualified group quickly decided that their report would be based on two sources: reports from eight diocesan agencies (e.g., Catholic school office, religious education department, Catholic social services) and grass-roots input.

The latter formed the more difficult task. How do you, from a practical standpoint, ask thousands of people to express their views on these topics? Once you work out those logistics, is it reasonable to expect much of a response from persons who have never before been publicly asked to share in such a delicate and serious decision? Will their observations be informed, prayerfully considered comments?

Despite a tight timetable and unclear answers to those questions, the committee believed the value of this process greatly outweighed any risks involved. As a result, it set up a procedure by which every Catholic in the diocese could participate in this praying, listening, reflecting, and speaking consultation. Publication of a special section in the diocesan paper, the *Catholic Sun,* served as the main vehicle for communication of the process.

Praying. A diocesan prayer and votive Masses were suggested, both excerpted from the Roman Missal in its section interestingly entitled "For the Election of a Pope or Bishop." In addition, a local Jesuit priest developed a prayer service for individual and group use.

Listening. Since the respondents should comment in an informed way with an appreciation of what the Church and office of bishop are or ought to be, the prayer service contained four readings. These texts—words of Jesus, St. Paul, Ignatius of Antioch and Vatican II Fathers—all touched on the function of a bishop and authority in Christ's Church. There were also references in the paper's special section to other appropriate biblical and conciliar passages.

Reflecting. A period of reflective silence after the prayers and readings was inserted hoping to insure that participants approached the consultation process with an attitude seeking to discern the Holy Spirit's movement within their own hearts and in the hearts of others.

Speaking. Participants had three ways of manifesting their opinions. Public hearings with the message tape-recorded and reproduced for the other committee members was one. Group discussion using a standard questionnaire, another. Individual completion of the same inquiry, the third. Results of the latter two were to be computerized.

The committee's final report, amended and approved by the Bishop's Senate, would then be forwarded to a number of appropriate individuals, including the Apostolic Delegate in Washington.

This wide-ranging, scriptural and prayer-oriented process and the document produced for that consultation are not the only factors determining the choice of a bishop. But they certainly should be one of them.

QUESTIONS FOR DISCUSSION

1. Describe the kind of model bishop you judge is needed to guide a diocese in the world today.
2. Suggest a few ways in which the people in a parish could sense a closer union with their bishop, e.g., blessing of the oils during Holy Week, Confirmation.

9 Vision of the Future

Pope John's Dream Coming True: The Dawn of a Golden Age

This section will predict a golden period for the Church during the next decade, the at least partial realization of a dream Pope John had when he summoned bishops for the Second Vatican Council. That venerable leader hoped for an inner renewal of the Church, a change of heart among Christians, a deepening of our spiritual lives. He also knew some fresh air was needed and called for those changes in structures or procedures necessary to bring the Catholic Church up to date and in tune with modern times.

What has happened since and, I think, is about to occur in the next few years, reflects the up-and-down, now peace, now persecution, first turbulent, then tranquil history of God's people in both Old and New Testament times. The Jews experienced persecution during days of the Maccabees, but they also remembered prosperity in earlier years within the Promised Land. So, too, the Church went underground in the first centuries, but then mushroomed, later, when given acceptance and freedom. Likewise, on the occasion of ecumenical councils, there customarily has been an ensuing period of turmoil, followed by some decades of tranquility.

Most readers probably have experienced our angry, painful post-Vatican II period. We have witnessed a remarkable number of changes within the Church—from such liturgical revisions as altars facing the people and vernacular, congregation participating rituals to institutional reforms like parish councils, team ministries and shared decision-making on various levels.

Those changes were not accomplished without a struggle nor were (or are) they universally accepted. Nevertheless, as indicated in several surveys, the heavy majority of American Catholics now have found them basically an improvement and given their support or endorsement. In the last several years this writer has lectured on the restored Rite of Penance all over the United States from Spokane to Clearwater and from San Diego to Fall River. Those many visits have given me an opportunity to catch the present mood of Catholics and sense the direction in which we are moving. That mood is highly encouraging and the direction very positive. For example, I have found crowds of both clergy and laity extremely serious and concerned about the interior conversion called for by the new ritual for reconciliation. Interest in prayer and sacred scripture likewise runs high. Most priests appear more settled and surer of their vocations. Students in Catholic institutions and public school religious education programs increasingly manifest a hunger for things of the Spirit.

It seems to me that the decade following the Vatican Council was filled with official (Vatican) and unofficial (grass-roots) efforts to modify the externals of the Catholic Church. People from above or below struggled to change traditional ways of praying and acting.

Instead of silent, Latin, priest-centered, rigid and uniform liturgies, the Church permitted a vernacular worship and asked for involvement by every member of the congregation in song, word and deed. Moreover, the new rituals offered a rich variety of texts and the freedom to adapt in a creative way liturgies to the diverse needs of various worshiping communities.

Similarly, instead of decisions by one person in isolation from others, processes have been established which entail shared decision-making, coresponsibility and wide-based consultation with all or at least representative members of the parish, diocese or universal Church. With these external procedures now fairly well in operation, Catholic Christians appear ready to plunge beneath them to the heart of the matter, to the inner growth these exterior processes are meant to facilitate.

I now would like to cite a few illustrations from around the country which indicate to me that such an era of inner reform and progress is already in its beginning stage and upon us.

- "I would ask you now to pause for a moment in silence praying that the Holy Spirit will inspire my words so they may be of some help to you."

Archbishop Raymond G. Hunthausen of Seattle made that request of 3,000 participants at a convention Mass during a Northwest Religious Education Institute.

This somewhat different introductory part of a homily brought complete silence (except for the repeated clicking of tape recorders being shut off by a few dozen persons). It was not, however, an unusual approach for this archbishop or for the other bishops in that section of our country.

These men gather bimonthly at a central location for a day of prayer and recollection; on the alternate months each bishop makes a similar day of his own.

Archbishop Hunthausen's request for prayer, his conscious dependence on the Holy Spirit, his spiritual attitude were not, then, out of character, but the natural result of such an intensified inner life. Moreover, these bishops have found their person-directed retreats and monthly recollection days have led them to other noteworthy actions, e.g., living in small apartments rather than large homes, feeling a greater concern for the poor and rejected of society, mixing more closely with both clergy and laity.

• Atonement Friar Dennis Sinnott operates the busy bookstore located at Graymoor on the Hudson River. The texts he finds in demand today are works on prayer and sacred scripture, a trend in sharp contrast to the popularity five to 10 years ago of action, conflict and speculatively theological publications.

• The Newark, New Jersey, archdiocesan liturgical commission and the Columbus, Ohio, diocesan religious education department recently sponsored workshops on the new Rite of Penance for priests, religious, teachers, religion coordinators and concerned lay persons.

The planners hoped for 600 in Newark; a crowd of 1,200 filled the auditorium. The Columbus committee planned on 500; over 800 arrived on the scene, necessitating a closed-circuit television arrangement in an adjacent hall for the overflow.

In both sessions, the audience listened with remarkably serious and sustained interest to a lengthy presentation on the revised ritual of reconciliation. This lecture sketched external modifications in the liturgy for Penance, but more importantly stressed the need for a radical change of attitude within both priest and penitent. Those in attendance seemed quite ready, even anxious, for that latter type of challenge.

• Many members of a tiny parish in the San Angelo, Texas, Diocese are deeply involved with the charismatic movement. It is not unusual for 50 of them to assemble at regular sessions, there reading God's word, sharing insights and praying with unique success for the healing of those suffering various ailments.

• High school students in religion classes are expressing a hunger for more doctrine in their courses, seem disposed to prayer experiences and appear unhappy with approaches which tend to be exclusively humanistic or social action oriented.

- On the refrigerator door in the home of a marriage encounter couple is a reminder for all in the family to pray on behalf of Mr. and Mrs. (Blank). This kind of praying for others has become a standard procedure for the father, mother and children in that family since they encountered six months ago. Their reaching out for others in such a prayerful fashion is not unique, but common to thousands of couples and families.

The Church and the Parish in 1987

A letter, received some time ago, certainly put my thinking processes into operation. At least it forced me to dream a bit, to ponder and try to predict the trends of our next decade.

The writer of the letter posed this question: "What do you think the Church will be in 1987 and, more specifically, where will liturgy be?"

My response follows, and with it the usual disclaimers which wise prophets of future events link to their predictions.

1. *"There will be increased and better pastoral planning on both the diocesan and parish levels."*

The very fact that your diocese is beginning to undertake some infant steps in the long-range pastoral planning process says something about what we can expect as this development matures. Moreover, the admirable effort of your own parish council to spend time now seeking to project what the parish will be like in 1987 indicates you already are where I look for most parishes to be 10 years hence.

This kind of "future shock" activity requires great discipline and effort on the part of parish leaders. Staff meetings and council deliberations must of necessity deal with many day-by-day problems. One slips easily, therefore, into a kind of hand-to-mouth pattern with plans sketched normally but for a few months and at most for a year in advance.

To step aside from those immediate concerns and spend a few hours a day or a week dreaming of what could and should be is difficult for all involved. The process bears much fruit, but it does not just happen; forward-thinking visionaries must make it happen.

Planning liturgies for a month or season of Sundays is a good practical measure along this path. Many parishes are doing it; perhaps most are not. The fact is that such an integration of homily, music and other elements greatly enhances the effectiveness of liturgical celebrations. That, too, however, demands discipline and effort.

We have found our annual report a useful occasion to summarize in spoken and published form the major achievements of the past and projections for the future. These are neither terribly long-range nor very comprehensive, but they do at least initiate the process of future pastoral planning.

2. *"We should see a better integration of the institutional and spiritual elements of the Church."*

Church history is one long series of attempts to steer a middle course between extremes. Truth rests there, of course, but we are inclined to be uncomfortable with that mysterious, gray, in-between, balanced position and seek the comfort of one side or the other.

The institutional Church of brick, mortar, laws, authority, obedience, externals dominated the scene prior to Vatican II. The spirit Church of cursillo, encounter, charism, freedom, spontaneity, feeling has come on heavily since the 1960's with its strengths and weaknesses.

Vision of the Future

I look for an increased awareness of the need for both elements in the complete Church of the 1980's.

For example, with care a good Eucharistic celebration can mix an "Agnus Dei" and a contemporary song from the theater, combine the proper proclamation of an official prayer and prayerful silence at various intervals throughout the Mass, and integrate repeated words or gestures (ritual) and creative artistic expressions of our inner faith.

3. *"It seems probable Catholic Christians in the 1980's will become more united within themselves and more alienated from the society in which we live."*

The latter may help foster the former.

Catholics were second-class citizens living in a ghetto complex before John Kennedy became President. Then, with his election and the developments of Vatican II, we became an accepted part of the nation, barriers broke down and seemingly America was one happy, religious family.

I have a feeling this has already begun to deteriorate. If so, we should not be too surprised. Certainly Jesus spoke often enough of his followers being persecuted, hated, rejected, etc.

To illustrate: the "entanglement" decisions of the national and state supreme courts as well as the abortion issue mean that certain traditional Catholic values and positions no longer receive support from the existing culture.

Thus, in the name of an impartial neutrality, schools in Florida may not consider Holy and Easter week as a basis for their calendar and vacations, state employees in California may not be released for Good Friday three-hour services, children in Virginia public schools may not be released from school for one hour of religious instruction.

One can debate whether these and other moves are just or unjust, good or bad for the country, helpful or hurtful for the Church. The truth is they have happened and more like them will probably occur in the next 10 years.

It does mean nevertheless that we cannot rely very heavily on society to reinforce the Church's teaching about Jesus, his life and his message. It likewise means we must adjust our parish programs accordingly.

4. *"I look for a balancing of the content and method approaches in religious education programs."*

Some marvelous steps have been taken over the past decade to reach particularly our young people by more contemporary and effective teaching methods. Audiovisuals, value clarification, fun activities, experience peaks, group discussion have tended to replace memorization and straight lectures.

Strangers to such programs will remark: "What has this to do with religion?" Those involved know these are but new means and tools to communicate ancient and traditional messages. Nevertheless there can be a tendency to become so enamored of the method that the content is overlooked.

With the developing trend I mentioned before, in which Christian Catholic values are less and less supported by the surrounding culture, we may see a greater need actually to teach or convey what are these truths and values, not merely clarify or deepen our awareness of them.

5. *"The traditional, territorial parish will remain the dominant unit of the Church, but complemented by personal affiliations and small worshiping communities."*

Predictions about the demise of territorial parishes run contrary to my observations here and around the country. Despite their many weaknesses, they will reach the greatest number of people and lasting or substantial progress in the Church ultimately depends on the progress of the traditional parish.

Vision of the Future 153

However, in these days of pluralism people should have the freedom to worship where they are most comfortable.

Our diocese has a long-established official policy by which individuals or families may affiliate through registration with any parish they wish. It does not bring about massive crossing of territorial lines, but offers a legitimate option for those seeking a special arrangement. It works so satisfactorily that I am surprised when I run into priests or dioceses with rigid territorial concepts of the parish. I expect our own approach will eventually become standard procedure in the nation.

In addition, floating, interest-centered, small-group worshiping communities connected to or separate from territorial parishes will probably continue to multiply, but never materialize as the main Christian cluster.

6. *"The importance of Sunday liturgies will become even more evident."*

Sundays have always been the day we reach most people in a parish. For the majority of Catholics, their only formal religious education after high school is the liturgy and the 10-minute homily. Moreover, the gradual secularization of con- of true principles.
temporary society means the weekly Eucharist must serve as a prime antidote for false values and a major communicator

This presupposes, of course, the allocation of prime time, personnel, energy and budget for carefully prepared and prayerfully executed Sunday liturgies.

7. *"Crucial moments of life will still be the best teachable opportunities and the occasions when Catholics and others are most disposed for a worship or religious experience."*

Birth, death, sickness, guilt, growth, love plus personal family, business, national and universal crises throw us into contact with the ultimate questions and mysteries of life. We are touched and troubled and turn to God for guidance and support.

Sensitive and concerned parishioners and parish leaders as well as liturgies which speak to these matters will have tremendous impact on those involved. The message of our Lord suddenly becomes personal and filled with meaning in such circumstances.

8. *"I expect the parental preparation programs for first reception of the sacraments, already quite common, will become more and more perfected and form probably the most effective adult religious education vehicle in a parish."*

Those of us who have introduced such projects know both the opposition and obstacles as well as the personal benefits and parish growth connected with these parental activities.

Once again, like an old record, if the prevailing culture does not underscore our basic Christian values, then the fundamental unit, the family, must assume an even greater responsibility in transmitting and preserving the Lord's word.

9. *"Catholic schools will probably have a less significant impact on the Church's life in the United States."*

The National Catholic Educational Association, in a recent report on the United States parochial school situation, gave, reluctantly and with heavy reservations, some highly tentative projections for 1979-80. Extension of those figures to 1984-85 offers us an indication that there will be about 1,000 fewer Catholic schools (elementary and secondary) with a total enrollment of approximately one million fewer pupils.

My own predictions here are quite ambivalent. Earlier comments I have made about Catholicism and an alien contemporary culture would lead me to believe that Catholic schools will be more necessary and desirable in 1987 than today. However, the astronomical costs, the dim prospect of state aid and the debilitating effect on the parish of huge assessments for school support make continued operation of those schools highly questionable from a financial viewpoint.

I do think that hard priorities must be observed. First we should budget for Sunday worship, next the total religious education program (adults and public school children), and only then the Catholic school. It seems to me that the order has normally been reversed in most parishes or dioceses prior to the present time.

10. *"Single persons and senior citizens should be offered greater consideration in the parish of 1987."*

I have previously stressed the critical importance of parental religious education programs. This reference to single persons and senior citizens does not conflict with that principle; it merely emphasizes the fact there will be an increasing number of these people in our parishes.

They, too, deserve our consideration, and ought to have special programs of their own. They should be carefully integrated into parish activities. Ask yourself now: How many are lectors, gift-bearers, parish council members, committee heads?

11. *"The permanent diaconate will take on an increasingly vital role in the life of American parishes."*

In lectures to these deacons and to candidates for that office at Paterson, New Jersey, Toledo, Ohio, and Tucson, Arizona, I have been very impressed by their goodness, enthusiasm and potential.

The future of the diaconate program seems without limit. The kind of work they will do, where they will labor, and how they will function are all uncharted areas. Sponsoring bishops and diocesan directors, to their credit, are surrounding the program with great freedom, allowing it to develop according to current needs coupled with the talents and status of the deacons.

12. *"Women will share more equally the leadership roles in parish functions."*

With Cardinal Suenens, I am not ready to predict Roman Catholic women priests in American parishes by 1987. However, we certainly can expect more and more women to serve as lectors, ministers of Communion, parish council representatives, religious education coordinators, co-pastors, pastoral assistants, etc.

13. *"I doubt, other than by exception, if there are married Roman Catholic priests by 1987 in the United States."*

Instead, I see the priest's function more restricted to worship leader, preacher, spiritual advisor with many previous tasks assumed by permanent deacons (married or single) and competent lay persons. Vocations to priesthood will probably increase slightly in number but the overall ratio of priests to lay persons will very likely decline.

Nevertheless, the more defined role will mean we need fewer priests, but priests of more unique talents and of greater holiness.

14. *"I foresee a great deepening of our Catholic prayer and faith life over the next decade."*

The liturgical books have now been reformed and we have available texts of great richness which require creative, prayerful, careful, faith-filled application to specific occasions and particular communities.

Less preoccupation with externals and more concentration on the inner reality of public worship and private prayer should mean a growing group of Catholic Christians who honor the Father in spirit and truth.

My list of predictions could go on, but these projections could help stimulate discussions about the Church in 1987.